Praise for
The Other Side of Wall Street

"Todd blows up the typical Wall Street stereotype and proves without a shadow of a doubt that nice guys can finish first. This book captures the essence of what it means to not only be a good trader, but to be a better person. If you read one book about Wall Street this year, this should be it."

—**Guy Adami,** CNBC's *Fast Money*

"Todd courageously reminds us that success in life isn't about what happened yesterday, or what may have occurred today—both good and bad—but what we are doing to make tomorrow better, despite it all. His journey is humbling and inspirational."

—**Peter Atwater,** President, Financial Insyghts LLC
and former Treasurer, Bank ONE

"Todd's unique combination of trader bravado and reflective sentimentality makes *The Other Side of Wall Street* a must-read for anybody who wants to go beyond the headlines to see how the financial world really works."

—**David Callaway,** Editor-in-Chief, MarketWatch

"Todd Harrison takes you on a high-speed train ride across a landscape inhabited by the financial wizards of our time. And he does it with his eyes wide open to the excesses and utility from an insider's point of view. This is real life played out to the hilt! Enjoy the ride...."

—**Bill Cella,** former CEO, Magna Global

"Fasten your seat belt as Todd Harrison takes you on a fast-paced and wild ride through the vicissitudes of his dramatic life. Harrison's gift for storytelling is on every page, and in the end, will bring a smile to your face."

—**William Cohan,** author of *Money and Power*

"Todd Harrison puts readers in the front row for a very personal story about his search for the true meaning of wealth. It moves beyond Wall Street headlines and sound bites, and provides an eye-opening account that covers one of history's most interesting market periods."

—**Michael J. Curcio,** President, E✱TRADE Securities LLC

"A personal history which parallels America's journey, from a country of real people and 'things' to an empire of monetary illusions and back again."

—**Satyajit Das,** author of *Traders, Guns & Money*

"Todd Harrison pulls back the curtain on Wall Street. Brutally honest and revealing about his life, this book gives us a fascinating and compelling insight into the pressures and politics of the world's financial capital and how one man tried to balance success and self-worth."

—**Martin Dunn,** former Editor-in-Chief, *New York Daily News*

"I found myself captivated and read the book in one night. Anyone with a dream should read this book as it's a true story of perseverance, determination, and dedication to doing what one loves."

—**Stephen Ehrlich,** Chief Executive Officer, Lightspeed Financial, Inc.

"A fascinating, entertaining, and honest account of a Wall Street insider who found his happiness as an author, entrepreneur, and philanthropist; it's a book every aspiring trader should read."

—**Marc Faber,** Editor, Gloom Boom & Doom Report

"A fascinating story. A behind-the-scenes look at the ups and downs of life through the eyes of a successful hedge fund trader and writer, as he learns about what really matters."

—**Bill Fleckenstein,** President, Fleckenstein Capital and author of *Greenspan's Bubbles*

"Todd Harrison has written a courageously thrilling account of his life on and off Wall Street. The book bristles with integrity, honesty, and personal confession; while being steeped in multimillion dollar spending on Long Island summer parties, Ferrari and Porsche boy toys, and a splash of expensive Bordeaux. A story of trading room power and busboy determination: It reveals what is behind the public facade of Wall Street."

—**Pimm Fox,** financial journalist and host of *Taking Stock* on Bloomberg TV and radio

"This isn't a book for trading tips—but an account of someone who figured out who he wanted to be in the world."

—**David Gaffen,** author of *Never Buy Another Stock Again*

"*The Other Side of Wall Street* provides an immensely personal, insider's view of the turbulent past decade on Wall Street. Todd Harrison chronicles his escape from the treadmill of hedge fund Hades to the wonderful world of Minyanville."

—**Steve Galbraith,** Partner, Maverick Capital

"In this moving memoir, Todd Harrison captures what it means to come of age on Wall Street. Meet the heroic and flawed characters who shape him along the way, from his grandfather and father to his former partner, Jim Cramer. Harrison is a brilliant trader with a poet's heart. He conveys the triumphant and tragic consequences of having an overwhelming desire to win and offers a nuanced tale of redemption and discovery."

—**Diane Galligan,** Managing Editor, Yahoo! Finance

"To read this book is to become emotionally involved in the journey of an incredibly talented, increasingly introspective, and articulate writer; but on a larger scale, it is about the journey we all share. As I read this book, I felt that Todd and I were sharing some possible answers to the question we all have: 'What is a good life?' There are lessons here for all of us."

—**Roger Goldman,** Chairman, Lighthouse International; General Partner, Berkshire Opportunity Fund; and ex-commercial banker

"…cathartic, candid, inspirational…"

—**Herb Greenberg,** Senior Stocks Commentator, CNBC

"Todd Harrison's trading made millions; his writing touched millions. His professional journey takes you inside three firms embedded in the zeitgeist of high finance in the late 20th and early 21st centuries, but its Todd's personal journey that makes this unlike any Wall Street story you have ever read."

—**Jamie Hammond,** former Business Editor, AOL and WashingtonPost.com

"Beautifully written, spoken from the heart. It's the best conversation about money at the personal and business level that I have ever read. It's tender, it's deep, and it touches you at many levels."

—**Dr. Tahira K. Hira,** Professor and Chairwoman,
NYSE Euronext Financial Literacy Advisory Committee

"Todd's evolution from Wall Street titan to digital thought leader and philanthropist is truly inspiring. I strongly recommend that people pick up the book and read his story firsthand."

—**Nick Johnson,** Digital Media Executive

"Like Jack Kerouac did almost 55 years ago, Todd Harrison offers a personal and iconoclastic journey that reveals an honest, lively, and visual spontaneity of style and content."

—**Douglas A. Kass,** President, Seabreeze Partners Management, Inc.

"*The Other Side of Wall Street* is certainly a hard book to put down! Todd Harrison does not tell us how we should live our own lives; he delivers an important message about what is important in life. Highly recommended!"

—**Peter E. Koveos,** Professor of Finance, Kiebach Chair in International Business,
Syracuse University

"Todd Harrison had a front-row seat on Wall Street's stunning two-decade roller coaster ride and played the game with best of them. It's a great read about a good guy who mixed street-smarts with bravado and rebirth in a spectacular fashion. and in the end, came out a mensch."

—**Larry Kramer,** Founder, Chairman, and CEO, CBS MarketWatch.com

"Todd has done a great job of giving a window into the fast-paced world of finance. It's great to be along for the ride, and doubly so because of the lessons learned along the way."

—**Larry Leibowitz,** Chief Operating Officer, NYSE Euronext

"Todd offers a rare vulnerability from a Wall Street insider with skill and humor. It is a tale that I am delighted to recommend to my friends, and one that will grab you and make you keep turning pages, just as it did to me."

—**John Mauldin,** four-time *New York Times* bestselling author
and President, Millennium Wave Investments

"What you do in this business when no one is looking is a story that needs to be told. Todd does so with transparency and accountability, and our profession should pay him a thank-you for that."

—**Keith McCullough,** CEO, Hedgeye Risk Management
and author of *Diary of a Hedge Fund Manager*

"With the cynicism many have about Wall Street, Todd Harrison reminds us that the machine is made up of people. From the pain and reckoning of witnessing 9/11 firsthand to inner conflict between ambition and compassion, Harrison's lens of the Street is overwhelming at times, enlightening, and a compelling read."

—**Don McPherson,** former NFL quarterback, College Hall of Fame quarterback,
and social education entrepreneur

"Harrison's extraordinary personal memoir is an emotional roller coaster of colossal wins and losses in the most tumultuous decade in investing history. Read these never-before-told stories from the hidden side of Wall Street—and welcome the author back to a better world."

—**Wenda Harris Millard,** President and COO, MediaLink LLC

"Todd Harrison's writing is at its enthralling best. He helps the reader find his or her own North Star and guideposts for a happy and meaningful life."

—**C. Warren Moses,** former CEO, The Children's Aid Society

"A brutally honest and gripping tale of life inside Wall Street's hottest and most dangerous institutions: giant investment banks and hedge funds. Harrison's journey to the center of the cyclone, and his discovery of the emptiness inside it, makes for a great read. It's a story of seduction and redemption, and has a plethora of great investment advice as a kicker."

—**Scott Patterson,** author of *The Quants*

"Ruby Peck—Todd's grandpa, my uncle—was an outsized character with a Cagney drawl, a tough-guy persona, and a mantra that penetrated to Todd's core: 'All you have is your name and your word.' At a time when financial types are viewed with equal doses of awe and scorn, *The Other Side of Wall Street* offers loving testimony to the need to find your soul in order to truly gain the world."

—**Abe Peck,** Director of Business to Business Communication,
Medill School of Journalism, Northwestern University

"In an age where financial chieftains gloat about doing 'God's work,' *The Other Side of Wall Street* should be required reading. A Walden for Wall Street, Todd shares a refreshingly honest and touching personal account of what it's like to claw to the top rung on the ladder of success, only to realize that you've actually distanced yourself from everything that counts."

—**Stephanie Pomboy,** President, MacroMavens LLC

"During the 1990s and 2000s booms and busts, few people showed greater insight as to how to navigate the currents than Todd Harrison. I have been waiting for years for him to tell the story of what he saw on the front lines of Wall Street, and he has finally spilled the beans! The straight dope from the last honest man on Wall Street...."

—**Barry Ritholtz,** author of *Bailout Nation*

"You never really learn anything in life by being lectured or told; you only learn through experience. Todd's powerful storytelling resonates in such a compelling way that we experience Wall Street from the comfort of our living rooms and gain insight as if we had experienced it firsthand."

—**Bobby Sager,** Chairman of the Board, Polaroid
and philanthropist

"Todd Harrison gives us the rare book about Wall Street and life that is both street-smart and forthright, one that acknowledges the seductiveness of money and sees clearly through it to what truly matters. With his characteristic passion, wit, honesty, and humanity, Harrison tells a story of professional success, personal trial, and the eventual redemption that comes with following one's principles and heeding one's heart."

—**Michael Santoli,** *Barron's* columnist

"Todd Harrison takes the reader along with him on his professional and personal journey, and shares the important lessons—both inspirational and instructive—that he learned along the way during both the go-go 1990s and the more sobering times that followed."

—**Gary Shilling,** President, A. Gary Shilling & Co., Inc.

"In a manner of speaking, Todd's life has been the market's real metaphor—unforeseen twists and turns, lots of volatility, and a long-term uptrend."

—**Steve Shobin,** Institutional Investor All-American Research Team
(1997–2000)

"An extraordinary personal adventure into the 'sanctum sanctorum' of Wall Street, this book is a rare chance to be an eyewitness to what really goes on in the leading brokerages and hedge funds."

—**Mason Slaine,** Chairman, President, and CEO,
Interactive Data Corporation

"Todd Harrison has seen it all, done it all, and earned perspective and insight available to only a few. If you want to know what it's really like at Wall Street's pinnacle—and in its deepest depths—this book will tell you."

—**Melvin T. Stith, PhD.,** Dean, Whitman School of Management,
Syracuse University

"Todd's adventure transcends political and professional boundaries; it's a tale of purpose and integrity in an age when those traits have become true commodities."

—**David Stockman,** Director of the Office of Management and Budget
(1981–1985)

"A great book for understanding what makes the market tick. A better book for understanding what makes people tick."

—**Aaron Task,** host of *The Daily Ticker*, Yahoo! Finance

The Other Side of Wall Street

In Business It Pays to Be an Animal,

In Life It Pays to Be Yourself

Todd A. Harrison

Vice President, Publisher: Tim Moore
Associate Publisher and Director of Marketing: Amy Neidlinger
Executive Editor: Jeanne Glasser
Editorial Assistant: Pamela Boland
Development Editor: Russ Hall
Senior Marketing Manager: Julie Phifer
Assistant Marketing Manager: Megan Colvin
Cover Designer: Freddy Hernandez
Managing Editor: Kristy Hart
Project Editor: Anne Goebel
Copy Editor: Geneil Breeze
Proofreader: Linda Seifert
Indexer: Lisa Stumpf
Senior Compositor: Gloria Schurick
Manufacturing Buyer: Dan Uhrig

© 2011 by Pearson Education, Inc.
Publishing as FT Press
Upper Saddle River, New Jersey 07458

FT Press offers excellent discounts on this book when ordered in quantity for bulk purchases or special sales. For more information, please contact U.S. Corporate and Government Sales, 1-800-382-3419, corpsales@pearsontechgroup.com. For sales outside the U.S., please contact International Sales at international@pearson.com.

Printed in the United States of America

First Printing June 2011

ISBN-10: 0-13-248966-X
ISBN-13: 978-0-13-248966-9

Pearson Education LTD.
Pearson Education Australia PTY, Limited.
Pearson Education Singapore, Pte. Ltd.
Pearson Education Asia, Ltd.
Pearson Education Canada, Ltd.
Pearson Educación de Mexico, S.A. de C.V.
Pearson Education—Japan
Pearson Education Malaysia, Pte. Ltd.

Library of Congress Cataloging-in-Publication Data:

Harrison, Todd A.
  The other side of Wall Street : in business it pays to be an animal, in life it pays to be yourself / Todd A. Harrison.
    p. cm.
  ISBN 978-0-13-248966-9 (hbk. : alk. paper)
  1. Harrison, Todd A. 2. Stockbrokers—United States—Biography. 3. Investment advisors—United States—Biography. I. Title.
  HG4928.5.H37A3 2011
  332.6092—dc22
  [B]
                              2011003038

For Ruby, Jamie, Gavin, Morgan…and Ruby.

"Gratitude unlocks the fullness of life.
It turns what we have into enough, and more.
It turns denial into acceptance, chaos into order,
confusion into clarity, problems into gifts,
failures into success, the unexpected into perfect timing
and mistakes into important events.
Gratitude makes sense of our past, brings peace for today,
and creates a vision for tomorrow."

—Melody Beattie

Contents

Foreword

Todd walked into my office a few months back and said, "I'm thinking of having these people write the foreword for my book." He rattled off a bunch of names—all of whom were good people worthy of writing the foreword. However, that wasn't my reaction. I looked at him with a blank stare and said, "Are you fucking kidding me?" I wasn't on the list. I've only known Todd for 25 years and have been his business partner for the last 6. Todd laughed uncomfortably and left the room. Now, I'm a relatively humble man, but I was pissed. A few minutes later, he came back and said, "Wow, you're right, it should be you. Would you please write the foreword?" I replied with a firm "NO."

Well, allow me to be...*forward*.

I write this with a tremendous sense of pride and honor. Todd labored over this book for some time, trying to strike a balance between too much information and the right amount to make it truly interesting for the reader. I listened and read and read and listened some more as he crafted this into something that I believe is of great interest to any reader. As I sit on a flight across country on behalf of Minyanville Media only a month before this goes to print, I have finally read the book cover-to-cover. While I had read bits and pieces before, I never read it in one sitting. I have to say that I couldn't put it down.

It's an invariable roller coaster that chronicles "the journey" that Todd and I have talked about throughout the years. And what a long, strange trip it's been.

When Todd labored over potential titles for the book, I participated in the process and finally recommending "In Business It Pays to Be an Animal, In Life It Pays to Be...." I couldn't finish the sentence, but with the help of Justin Rohrlich we arrived at "In Life It Pays to Be Yourself." And there is was—the perfect title, a statement that hit on both sides of trying to attain riches while trying to figure life out.

Todd's an interesting cat. I've known him since 1987. It's hard to say that year out loud; it's close to a quarter century, and we've had quite a journey. Our friendship started back in college and continued through my time in Hollywood and his time on Wall Street, and each year we made it a point to get together on either coast. Todd has a way about him. He is a force of nature with a gravitational pull. He has a unique ability to pull people into his sphere and make them part of the *journey*. It's only with hindsight and this book that I realize how integral I have been to this.

Back in 2001 when Todd told me he was starting this Web site, he asked if I would speak with the person he had hired to create the platform. I spent countless hours at night and on weekends talking on the phone, suggesting ideas and potential partners to produce a Web site for what would become Minyanville. He certainly spared no expense hiring the best of the best to bring his vision to life, and it's when that vision took on a life of its own that it became a truly viable business. It was in 2004 when I had that epiphany. I always wanted to "have skin in the game"—to be an entrepreneur. Minyanville provided me with that opportunity.

I had spent the seven previous years building a $20 million organization for J. Walter Thompson called digital@jwt. It was time to shift from being the intrepreneur to an entrepreneur, and when Todd presented the opportunity in August 2004, I was in.

It was scary. I had many discussions with my wife before taking the leap—we had two young sons—but the idea was just too good. My wife said, "Let's do it." So I called Todd and said, "Let's brand the Bull and Bear of Wall Street fame and effect positive change through financial understanding." It sounded easy enough but wow, were we wrong. It wasn't—and still isn't—easy.

I'm guessing when Walt Disney walked into his first presentation and said (hopefully not in the voice of Mickey Mouse), "I'm going to take two mice and make them the ambassadors for happiness," people said he was nuts. And trust me, we have walked out of meetings where the person we presented to has said, "You're nuts! Good luck."

Then there are those we've presented to who have looked at what we're doing and had the same eureka moment I had when Todd first wrote from the perspective of Hoofy the bull and Boo the bear.

Brilliant! People like Larry Kramer, founder of MarketWatch, or Wenda Millard, president of Medialink, or Charlie Managno who ran global marketing for Merrill Lynch for 16 years. They saw it. They got it. They get it. And it's only a matter of time until others "get it." Todd has always been early.

It's hard to write about a best friend because even though you've read the text on the pages, you've also lived the movie alongside him through the ups and downs, wins and losses, and happiness and heartache. It often becomes a blur or montage of memories, and it takes a bit of work to fit the pieces of the puzzle back together.

Through it all, Todd has proven time and time again that the glass is always half full. He's someone who can turn obstacles into opportunities with a resolve that's unmatched. He looks at the bright side of life, and that's what makes him a special individual.

This book is worth reading because it provides a rare glimpse of someone who has been inside the Wall Street machine and has been chewed up and spit out only to jump back in time-and-time again to disprove the naysayers and doubters. It will inspire people to truly think about what's important to them as they try to navigate a chaotic world, live life to the best of their ability, make money, be true to family, but more importantly, to be true to themselves and find some semblance of balance.

The Other Side of Wall Street ends with Chapter 18 aptly titled "The Journey," but there are now another dozen chapters since the book was written, a new addition to Todd's family since it went to print, and countless changes positive and negative in Minyanville Media's evolution. There will be dozens more to follow.

Todd Harrison and Minyanville Media have been years in the making, but truth be told, the journey has only just begun.

Kevin Wassong
May 2011

Preface

I never thought I was *that guy*. Despite having spent much of my career pursuing money, I always believed that I was a good man who lived life with an honorable ethos. My grandfather had taught me that all you have is your name and your word, and that honesty, trust, and respect were the foundational elements of any successful endeavor. While I remained true to those lessons, I ultimately fell prey to the false idolatry of money in my quest for the bigger, better thing.

This is a story of personal experience, although none of what you're about to read comes from a place of perceived accomplishment. I'm not particularly proud of some of the details in the pages that follow, but they helped shape the person I am today.

I confused net worth with self-worth.

I didn't know the difference between having fun and being happy.

I looked for validation in the bottom of a bank account and when I arrived at where I thought I wanted to be, I wanted—and *needed*—more.

It would have been easy to identify those mistakes with the benefit of hindsight, particularly after the financial crisis brought an age of austerity to bear, but my clarity arrived more than a decade ago when a confluence of events altered my perception and triggered an awareness—or what some might call an introspective redemption.

As much as I thought I understood my choices in life and the ramifications thereof, it was difficult to appreciate how they affected others. I was reminded of that in the summer of 2010 while spending a few days with my brother Adam during his annual "guys" weekend at the beach. I intended to spend the majority of my time working on this book; it's funny how inspiration arrives when you're not looking for it.

Peter Emanuel, who was at the time on staff as a scientist at the White House and had been a fraternity brother of Adam's during their days at the University of Maryland, sat next to me on an outdoor bench following dinner and a game of pool. Peter and I had known each other for more than 20 years, but we never really *knew* each other.

As we chatted on that random night, he turned to me and said, "You know, I never liked you very much. You made me feel insignificant for a very long time; it was degrading." He recalled a story in 1997 when he and Adam visited me in New York City for Halloween, and we went to some swanky upscale club.

"You walked in wearing an expensive shirt; the bouncers immediately greeted you and ushered us past the line and upstairs, past another bouncer into a private room. You ordered a round of $10 martinis, and beautiful girls surrounded you. I was a scientist trying to cure cancer; $10 was my entire dinner budget. What's worse, you seemed to revel in it; you appeared to enjoy the status and aura, ambivalent to those outside your inner circle. You never knew this, but that night inspired me. It motivated me to work harder. I never again wanted to feel that small."

Peter and I also discussed how September 11th was a major catalyst for us both. For me, it led to a personal, professional, and spiritual transformation—a journey to effect positive change. For him, it was a steppingstone in what continues to be a meaningful pathway in life. We bonded that night, connecting in a way we never had before— perhaps in a way that I wasn't open to years prior.

I never knew Peter felt that way, nor had I ever seen myself in that light, but I imagine he wasn't the only one. While I thought I was savoring life and living in the moment, I came across as an arrogant ingrate who never appreciated, or was satisfied with, what I had.

I never thought I was that guy.

1

The Age of Innocence

It's a rare occurrence when you can exhale, relax, and enjoy your good fortune. That was the case at the end of 2000 after our company posted a monster year. Cramer Berkowitz, of which I was president, had already earned a reputation as a shrewd and honest hedge fund, and I had money in the bank as tangible validation of my hard-fought year. I wrote the trading diary for TheStreet.com and had settled into a seamless rhythm of running the trading operation at a $400 million fund while sharing my stream of consciousness in real-time for the world to see.

Yet there were pressures in other areas of my life. My grandfather, Ruby, grew increasingly ill, and he was spending much of his time in intensive care. It was an anxious time for my family as we readied ourselves to say goodbye to our patriarch; it was a dose of reality in an otherwise excellent stretch. Ruby had been a major influence throughout my life. He was more than my guiding light; he was my hero.

My dad left our family when I was two years old, and my grandfather assumed his role. As wonderful as my mother was, devoting herself to raising her children, a young boy needs a man in his life to set the tone and set him straight. As I grew older, I learned that everything happens for a reason. Divorce can be difficult for a child, but it facilitated a bond that might not otherwise exist. Ruby's presence was empowering, and we became best friends. He taught me how to be a man.

When I graduated college in 1991 and started at Morgan Stanley, I couldn't afford an apartment in New York City. The confidence that defined my Syracuse University experience had suddenly morphed into an exposed vulnerability as I attempted to learn a craft. I needed a beacon for my moral compass, and, luckily, I didn't have to look far.

I lived in the den of my grandparents' home on the upper east side of Manhattan as I found my way. I was overwhelmed with trying to understand the complexities of the financial markets, but I could always count on one thing: Every time I turned around and whenever I needed assurance, Ruby was there with a knowing glance and a steady hand.

Years later, my grandmother, Dorothy, told me that my grandfather sat in my room while I was at work and stared at my shoes. "He loved you so much," she said with a smile, "he just wanted to be closer to you."

I was too naive to understand the golden door that opened when I started on Wall Street—or the cost it would exact through the years—but what I lacked in experience was supplanted by my grandfather's guidance, and I promised myself that I would never let down the single most important person in my life.

His phrases struck a chord and lit the way, even if I didn't fully appreciate the magnitude of their meaning.

Earning stripes on the Morgan Stanley equity derivative desk, as I did after college, wasn't easy. I knew very little about the business, but thanks to my grandpa, I was well-versed in how to conduct myself as a human being. I had spent countless hours sitting by his side as he espoused wisdom that transcended generations or chosen fields:

"All you have is your name and your word."
"What goes around comes around."
"Time is the most precious of commodities."
"Think positive."

His phrases struck a chord and lit the way, even if I didn't fully appreciate the magnitude of their meaning. Each step of my career ushered in a new set of challenges that made my previous plateau pale in comparison, but every time I stumbled, which happened often, Ruby was there to pick me up and point me in the right direction.

When he became ill in 2001 and was admitted to the Delray Medical Center, I traveled to Florida most weekends so I could hold his hand as he struggled. After numerous readers of my column e-mailed to joke about how I was slacking off in the Hamptons, I shared the tale of Ruby. I wrote about why he mattered, where he was, and how very much I loved him.

An amazing thing began to happen. I received e-mails and letters from around the world from people who shared similar stories about grandparents, children, mothers, fathers, and fallen friends. There were ten at first and then a hundred. In time, there were *thousands*. We read those tributes to Ruby while he lay in intensive care, one after another, month after month.

If so many people took the time to write someone they never met to lift the spirits of a man they had only read about, I pledged that I would continue to share my insights in an attempt to help them navigate the twists and turns of the financial universe. That effort was the genesis of a loyal community that remains to this day, and it was then I realized the power of the Internet, the catharsis of writing, and the importance of giving back.

As I prepared myself for a devastating loss, I settled into my role as a "trader who writes," and the irony wasn't lost on me. I was the president of Cramer Berkowitz, and I wrote the trading diary on

TheStreet.com, both of which were positions previously held by Jim Cramer. A little more than a year earlier, when he and I had finalized the terms of our partnership, I had no idea why someone would fragment his or her professional focus by writing during the trading day. Yet there I was, producing more than a dozen short-form articles on a daily basis and balancing those seemingly disparate skill-sets.

The relationship between Jim and me was buffered on both sides by business and money. He had invested a large portion of his money in the fund and left it there after he retired, which served as a tacit stamp of approval, while I managed the risk with Jeff Berkowitz and Matt Jacobs and generated page views for TheStreet.com. We had a vested interest in keeping each other happy, and despite a persistent yet unspoken tension, we did just that.

In March 2001, three months after Jim retired from the firm, United Cerebral Palsy honored me for outstanding achievement. I was unsure why I was chosen to receive the award but assumed that they thought my presence would drive attendance. With the help of my friend Steve Nitkin, I secured Run-DMC to perform and then reached out to brokers on the Street to whom we paid commission. Not surprisingly, we sold out the event and raised a lot of money for a worthy cause.

During the ceremony, Cramer stepped on stage and lauded me as the best trader on Wall Street and the best writer at TheStreet.com. I didn't agree with his assessment, but that was Jim—over the top and all or nothing. I smiled in a knowing and familiar way; while our professional relationship was strained, I genuinely cared for the man and understood why he acted the way he did.

As it turned out, that speech was the apex of our personal relationship.

Saying Goodbye and Opening Up

It was a random Wednesday in the spring of 2001 when I suddenly stopped trading and booked a flight. I *knew* something was wrong and rather than wait for my scheduled sojourn that Friday, I canceled my appointments and headed south. I arrived at the hospital, raced to my grandfather's room, held his hand, and whispered in his ear. Five minutes later, a rush of energy passed through my body, limb by limb and goose bump by goose bump, as his body shut down and his grip softened. It was his time, and he passed on his terms, surrounded by his family as he had wished.

A few weeks prior, during one of my visits, he briefly regained consciousness and whispered in my ear, "Take care of the family." Other than a tender moment with Dorothy, his loving wife of 59 years, when he told her she looked beautiful, those were the last words he would ever speak. He was a boxer in his youth, and I assume he fought until he knew we were ready to let go. I should have been prepared for the pain, but that reality was harsh. Letting go is one thing, but navigating the world without a north star would be entirely more profound.

People deal with loss in different ways. For me, it meant honoring his memory and staying true to the man that he taught me to be. They say the greatest tribute you can pay someone is living your life in a manner consistent with what he or she would have wanted. Soon after his passing, I launched the Ruby Peck Foundation for Children's Education to channel his energy to future generations.

Denial, anger, sadness, bargaining, and acceptance, as defined by Kübler-Ross, are widely considered to be the five stages of grieving. I had emotionally prepared as best I could, and when he finally passed, I edged into a state of sadness and readied to face the world alone. A video tribute that featured my grandfather was played the night of the UCP benefit, and he said, "I don't know if I taught him a lot, but I sure hoped he learned a lot." He did and, by extension, so did I.

My grieving process threaded into my column on TheStreet.com. My editors allowed for some latitude, but it was clear that they wanted nuts and guts financial stuff and would put up with only so much human interest. An underlying tension began to emerge as their editorial staff carved up my columns before they posted. I never claimed to be a good writer, but I spoke from the heart and told the truth. Sometimes, a word here or a shift there can change the entire complexion of the content. I bit my lip as they explained proper grammatical execution to me, and my eyes darted around my eight screens attempting to synthesize hundreds of millions of dollars of risk.

My inbox filled daily with hundreds of e-mails, many of which were about the markets, but a surprising number of which had nothing to do with the tape. It amazed me how diverse my audience was, but, upon reflection, it made complete sense. They weren't traders who happened to be human beings; they were human beings who happened to be traders.

The Critters Cometh

I used metaphorical representations to represent the stock market—Hoofy the Bull and Boo the Bear—and told both sides of the trading story. There was always a bull case and a bear case, I thought at the time, and the residual grist was what the financial media reported the following morning. It made sense to write through that lens and examine the friction between opinions, which was where I believed true education was found. In time, my readers asked what Hoofy was doing or what Boo was thinking, and they began to assume personalities and perspectives. They resonated—people *liked* them. It occurred to me that nobody had ever branded the Wall Street bull and bear.

Hoofy the Bull and Boo the Bear.... There was always a bull case and a bear case....

TheStreet.com paid me a salary—$100,000 a year—but it paled in comparison to the money I made running a large fund. For me, writing wasn't about the compensation as much as it was the catharsis, and we never signed a contract because I didn't believe TheStreet.com should own the words "Hoofy" or "Boo." That legal language was industry standard at the time, but it wasn't my primary industry, nor was it my standard.

They didn't press the issue; to them, I was a cash cow that produced content, a man in the trenches who generated page views. I wrote incessantly as I navigated the other side of the technology bubble and chronicled my trades for the world to see. If the stock market was a casino, it felt like I had the dice in my hands for an incredibly long time. TheStreet.com was happy, our investors were happy as we notched double-digit gains, and I was happy, albeit a bit hollow. Profitability was a wonderful distraction from the pain of losing my grandfather, but it didn't fill the void.

Life was good, or so I thought, as I had the toys that society bestows on those with wealth. Forget all the time that elapsed while I sat in front of my screens in an attempt to make money. There would be more dinners with friends, plenty of time to find a bride, and countless hours to relax.

Summer Loving

The loss of my grandfather notwithstanding, life had never been better, at least as measured through a monetary lens. While others struggled with the fire sale on Wall Street, our fund made big money, and I lived the lifestyle to prove it. My buddy Lionel and I ventured to the Hamptons to look for a summer rental in my brand new BMW M5, which I had bought a few weeks prior without so much as looking at the sticker price.

A broker from Sotheby's had called to tell us of a house in Sag Harbor that had to be seen, and the moment we drove into the compound, we knew it was perfect. "We'll call it Ruby Ridge," I said before we got out of the car to explore the grounds.

It was sensational. The Philippe Starck-designed house was stocked with Lichtensteins and featured a meditation tower, a media room, and a wraparound terrace that overlooked Sag Harbor. There were immaculate rolling grounds with an eight-car garage, an adjacent two-bedroom casita, and an outdoor dining pavilion with a working fireplace and kitchen that surrounded a black gunite pool. A croquet field sat between the compound and a 200-foot private beach, all within walking distance of town.

"Seven bedrooms," one of us said, "there's a lot of space here." The broker told us the house was listed at $150,000 for the summer, and it was ours before we got back into my car. We pulled in five or six friends, turned the garage into a nightclub called Shagababy, and smiled amongst ourselves when we eventually overheard others talking about the new, private club somewhere in Sag Harbor.

There were hundreds of people at Ruby Ridge on any given weekend, and we partied like rock stars through the night. It was a summer of debauchery straight out of a movie, a twisted tale of revelry that could have been called "The Top of the Market." As a trader with my finger on the pulse of trends and turns, I should have seen disaster coming from a mile away.

I left for Hawaii on Labor Day weekend to fulfill a promise I had made to my father, that if he stayed clean, I would return the next year to enjoy quality time with him. He looked good when I saw him; he was off drugs, and his condition was properly medicated. He had volunteered at an animal refuge and proudly walked me through the grounds while I was there.

As we talked about life and the ways of the world, he was eager to hear about my journey, what I was doing on Wall Street, and more importantly, if I was happy. "Sure," I said as we sat by the pool at the Four Seasons Hotel. "I'm the President of a $400 million dollar hedge fund, I made millions of dollars last year, and I've got everything I could ever want absent my own family, which is only a matter of time."

I suppose we were anxious to impress each other, albeit for different reasons. I yearned for parental acceptance after years of feeling like a substandard son while he, in his own words, wanted to make me proud of how he climbed out of his own abyss. In the end, our motivations didn't really matter; I had a father again, and the week passed quickly.

The night before I returned to New York, we sat at an outdoor restaurant that overlooked the ocean as a gentle Maui breeze made for a perfect backdrop. I'll never forget the last thing he said to me before the check came, as I shared my future aspirations. "Relax, son, and enjoy life; you never know when a plane will fall out of the sky and ruin your day."

The following Tuesday was September 11th, but before I get to that, perhaps I should start at the beginning....

2

Bagel Boy

I was two years old when my father left and three years old when we transitioned from a large house in New Jersey to a small apartment in Great Neck, Long Island. The world as I knew it had turned upside down; we lived in a new town, my dad was gone, my mother worked all day, and it seemed like someone else took care of me every other day. It was a confusing time, with rapidly conflicting emotions.

Looking back, my parents' marriage, a fast-tracked union facilitated by the Vietnam War during a time of intense geopolitical uncertainty, was doomed from the start. None of that mattered to a toddler; we were one of three divorced families in the town, and my childhood felt anything but normal.

My mother was a kindergarten teacher but took a marketing job in Manhattan to make ends meet. I give her a lot of credit; she insisted that her job be commission-based so that she could set her schedule around the needs of her children. My brother Adam and I shared a room and adapted to life without a father, while our mom balanced her responsibilities. Her income, along with help from my grandparents, afforded us a lower middle-class existence, and for all intents and purposes, we had a loving home.

Our apartment was a few blocks from the railroad station, on the sixth floor and overlooking a park, and while we lived in an affluent town, it wasn't the wealthiest of neighborhoods. Great Neck was a place where children measured each other by the logo on their shoes and labels on their shirts. That was my first taste of money, having some, but seemingly never having enough.

"If you want more money, get a job."

When I visited friends on the other side of town, I marveled at the sprawling lawns and fancy cars. I asked my mom why we lived with such modest means, unaware of how painful it must have been for a single parent with two young boys to field such questions. Her response was always the same—*"If you want more money, get a job."*

My dad had moved to California, and our interaction was limited to infrequent visits, phone calls, and years later, occasional summers. I would stare at the phone on my birthday waiting for it to ring, looking for a semblance of normalcy or an inkling of paternal acceptance. It rarely if ever did, and that affected me in ways that would take years to comprehend.

My dissatisfaction manifested in many ways, which was magnified by the fact that I was diagnosed with ADHD at a young age. Starved for attention, I got into fights and lashed out at whoever got in my way. I yearned for validation, and when it didn't arrive, I drained milkshakes to satiate my hunger. I was overweight and underliked, which is a difficult dynamic for any child to navigate. The Ritalin I was prescribed kept me awake most nights, and I sat outside my mother's door listening for sounds, hoping she was also awake so she could keep me company.

I didn't fit in socially, and by the sixth grade, it was clear that changes needed to be made. My mother met with social workers and tried to identify a positive pathway for her youngest child. I was eventually removed from the public system and placed in a school located in Jamaica, Queens, that focused on children with special needs through smaller classes.

While that was a necessary step, I didn't understand it at the time. I grew more aggressive, got into fights, and rebelled whenever possible. The issue wasn't intelligence—I received "post high school" grades on many of my mandatory tests—it was behavioral. I knew one thing—I hated the fact I didn't attend public school and craved normalcy; I just wanted to fit in.

By seventh grade, I realized that if there was going to be a change, it needed to start within. I wrote my dream on a piece of paper—the class schedule at the public school—with a note underneath that read, "Please God, let it be true." Other students taunted me and my initial instinct was to fight, but I realized that would only push my dream farther away. I focused on change, put my best foot forward for the remainder of the year, and the following autumn, I enrolled in Great Neck South Middle School.

I worked at the local bagel shop at the age of 13, the first job of continual employment that continues to this day, and awoke at 5:00 a.m. on Saturdays to prepare for the mad rush of customers, including many of the families I aspired to emulate. *If you want more money, get a job.* I'll never forget the symbolism of that counter, a marble divide representing the chasm between the haves and have-nots as money changed hands for goods and services. Little did I know that I would experience life on both sides of that cash register, and little did I know that I should have been careful what I wished for.

When I was back in the public school system, my ADHD persisted, as did the aggressive tendencies. My mother had the foresight to guide me toward sports so I could channel my energy in a positive direction. I progressed as an athlete—what I lacked in skill, I made up for with effort—and had finally settled into a normalized, somewhat traditional childhood.

West LA Fade Away

The void that was left when my father disappeared was powerful. On the rare occasions that I saw him, he seemed "foggy" and distant, and there was often a funny odor that I wouldn't place until much later in life.

I visited him in Woodland Hills, California, during the summer a few times as a child. He was in the post-production business, and he evidently made a decent living. He had a home in the hills, a pool in the backyard, and expensive cars in the garage. There were times we connected—times I cherished—but his mood was volatile and our relationship inconsistent. I recall one episode when I was about ten. As we walked through the garage after a swim in the pool, I told him that my biggest fear in life was ending up like him. He took a swing at me as I slipped to the ground; he missed, but I began to cry with hopes he wouldn't come down with a second shot.

Adam and I were typical siblings; we fought a lot in our youth, but an underlying love rooted our relationship. One morning in Great Neck, I awoke to find him sitting in his bed, crying and petting our cat Valentino. I asked what was wrong and he told me to go back to sleep. When I was at school the next day, his friends told me that he had moved to California, and I returned home to find our mother screaming into the phone at our father.

Adam had made decisions in an attempt to address his own issues—feelings I was unaware of at the time—and returned east at the end of his junior year after my father separated from his wife, one of his six marriages to five different women. Ruby flew out to retrieve Adam after my brother told him that he was scared of our father's potential reaction; while we were both young, we knew, even at that age, that nobody fucked with Ruby.

After a childhood of trying to find and understand myself, I lost considerable weight when I was 14. Between playing sports, developing friendships, and dating, if we can call it that, I reached an internal equilibrium when I applied myself and was rewarded for my efforts. High school can be a vicious place, particularly in Long Island where you're often judged by possessions. My self-esteem was fragile—I felt responsible for my father's absence, like my arrival to the world somehow chased him away. I tried to reconcile my abandonment issues, but the needle kept pointing inward. While I had everything I hoped for at the time—everything I had wished for years prior—something tangible was missing.

My father and I communicated with increased frequency, and as I was about to enter my junior year of high school, I wanted to find out who he was and decided to move to southern California. While my mother wasn't thrilled with my decision, she understood that it was something I needed to do and a lesson I must learn for myself. I had to answer the questions that continued to plague me.

I packed my belongings and headed west.

The Swing Vote

My father's energy vacillated from one day to the next and our encounters were random—one moment we were tossing a baseball and trying to recapture lost time, and the next I tiptoed through the house because he was upset and I didn't want him to hear me. I thought he was moody, but years later I discovered something entirely more disturbing. He suffered from something beyond his control and foreign to what was understood by society at that time.

One evening, my dad pulled into the driveway in a flashy red Ferrari and announced he had been promoted at work. I'll never forget how much he loved that car. He washed, waxed, and detailed it as if it alone was symbolic of his success. He enjoyed the attention as he drove through town, and I suppose I did as well. I would witness that stretch for status many times when I eventually arrived on Wall Street.

I also bought a car, a red Nissan 200SX, as I was eager to emulate him. My father cosigned the loan with the understanding that I would be responsible for the monthly payments. I worked several consecutive jobs to satisfy that obligation; I worked at a New York Deli at the local mall, managed a Subway down the street from my high school, and traveled to Simi Valley to pick weeds for 50 bucks a day. My mother's advice played often in my head. *"If you want more money, get a job."*

When that wasn't enough, I sold the baseball card collection that my grandfather had given to me. Mickey Mantle, Babe Ruth, Willy Mays, and a vintage Bob Gibson were a small price to pay for extra cash, or so I thought. I missed playing sports but was willing to make the sacrifice if it meant having wheels. California was a lot different from New York. If you didn't have a car, you weren't in the game. It simply wasn't an option.

One night, in the middle of my senior year, my father walked into my room and told me that he got fired from his job and had to sell his Ferrari. He said he needed my car to go on interviews, but I still had to make the payments. If I didn't like it, he said, I could follow in my brother's footsteps and move back to Great Neck. I agreed to his plan, hoping to help him get back on track, or that was my post-rationalization. I suppose the truth was that I didn't want to be abandoned again, or be banished as the case may be, and I did whatever it took to avoid that outcome.

I finished the school year, worked to make the car payments, and applied to several colleges on the west coast, including UC–Santa Barbara and San Diego State. I also applied to east coast schools such as Boston University and Syracuse. While I enjoyed the California weather, I was a New Yorker at heart, and I wanted to be closer to the other side of my family.

My lone goal was to be on the other side of the cash register.

Shortly after graduating Taft High School in 1987, I returned east and worked as a short-order cook in Times Square the summer before my freshman year. I paid close attention to the well-dressed professionals who scurried to work and rarely, if ever, made eye contact with the young man in a white apron behind the counter. As I readied for a fresh start in upstate New York, it was hard to contain my excitement.

My lone goal was to be on the other side of the cash register.

3

Animal House

I walked onto the Syracuse University campus knowing nobody and excited for a fresh start. It was an expensive institution, but the efforts of my mother, support from my grandparents, financial aid, and work-study programs made the experience possible. Syracuse was everything I wanted in a college: a quality education, an expansive campus, a thriving Greek system, and a nationally prominent athletic program.

There were a few familiar faces from Great Neck, but nobody I would consider a friend. That changed the first day of classes when I walked into Sociology 101 in the Maxwell Auditorium. As I sat in the fishbowl-style classroom, a shaggy-haired kid with a Zeta Psi hat was sitting directly in front of me. He was drawing a picture-perfect Tasmanian Devil, and my eyes drifted to his handiwork.

"That has to be traced," I offered as we gathered our books, opening a conversation. "Nope, it's freehand," he said with a smile while extending his hand. "I'm Kevin Wassong, sophomore—damned glad to meet you!" We continued to talk as we walked out of the building, and I watched him converse with other students. He had a way about him, an infectious energy that combined the easiness of Andy Dufresne in *The Shawshank Redemption* and the innocence of Kevin Arnold from *The Wonder Years*. It's safe to say that he was instantly likable.

Our friendship grew throughout my first semester, and I pledged Zeta Psi that spring. The following year, we roomed together in our fraternity house, continued to build upon our bond, and by the time we broke for the summer, we were best friends. He joined me for a vacation to southern California the following year, and we stayed with my dad in Long Beach, where he was living with spouse number four in a small house in a bad neighborhood. We actually heard gunshots as we sat on the front porch talking about our future plans. The next day, we ventured to Universal Studios to take the tour, and I immediately saw a gleam of excitement in his eyes.

When Kevin graduated in 1990, he landed a job at the Creative Artists Agency in Los Angeles and pursued his passion for entertainment. While he earned a degree from the Newhouse School of Communication and I studied business management, we always talked about working together one day. Twenty years later, we would do just that.

As I made my way through Syracuse University, I wanted to study business but wasn't sure of which major to pursue. I enjoyed accounting, but finance seemed entirely more exciting—one industry created wealth and the other simply counted it. I reminded myself that if I wanted to make money, I needed to stand near the cash register. The deepest drawers were on Wall Street, I knew, but I didn't have blue blood or a means of infusion. That posed a problem unless I could somehow identify a way to crack the code. I had to think outside the box.

The deepest drawers were on Wall Street, I knew, but I didn't have blue blood or a means of infusion.

I was a good student who took my academic career seriously, despite an active commitment to collegiate hedonism. I was competitive in part because I felt that I had something to prove. When I viewed coursework as a contest, I started to pull away from my peers. Graduating with honors was a good start, but I knew that it wouldn't be enough when I began to interview at Wall Street firms.

I wanted more, the fatal flaw of a classic overachiever.

I waited tables my freshman year at the local Bennigan's and used those tips to underwrite a bartending class the following summer. I worked at several bars when I returned to school before landing a job during my junior year as a bouncer at Harry's, one of the more popular hangouts on the hill. I had no interest in standing outside in the Syracuse chill, but it was an opportunity to get my foot in the door—that too would provide a valuable lesson that came in handy later in life.

When the regular bartender called in sick one night, I was asked to replace him, and under the watchful eye of the owner, I was "high ring," putting more money in the till than the older, more experienced pourers. I then joined the starting rotation and with each successful night, I was given more latitude. In a few short months, I had my choice of shifts.

I had everything that I could have ever dreamed of. I bartended at my favorite watering hole, excelled in my class work, enjoyed fraternity life, and did the types of things that college kids wanted to do. I had it all, yet I wanted more, the fatal flaw of a classic overachiever.

The Ace of Spades

During my junior year, I aced my finance midterm and blew the bell curve. Pride would have been an appropriate reaction, but I studied the few wrong answers and loathed the lack of perfection. That was my style—set the bar too high so if I missed, I would still be ahead of the crowd. It wasn't the healthiest approach, as I never allowed myself to feel a true sense of accomplishment.

Following the test, my finance professor called me to his office. As I walked across the campus to accept his praise, I allowed myself a rare moment of satisfaction. Things were going well and despite the looming unknown of what I would do after graduation, I let myself enjoy that moment as I raced across the quad on that frigid Syracuse afternoon.

When I arrived, he proceeded to grill me on the subject matter, one question after another, as he stared into my eyes. After a few minutes, I realized what was happening.

"You think I cheated?" I asked, calmly at first but then with increased agitation. "I busted my ass for this class, and you're accusing me of cheating?"

Following an intense exchange, the conversation eased into a healthy dialogue, and, as fate would have it, the professor oversaw the Department of International Programs Abroad. There were several internship opportunities available overseas that summer, most of which were geared toward MBAs. He began to gauge my interest as I asked which companies participated in the program. He listed them one by one: Manufacturer's Hanover. Saatchi & Saatchi. Morgan Stanley....

"Morgan Stanley?" I interrupted, recognizing the name of one of the biggest cash registers on the Street. "If I can intern at Morgan, I'll gladly hop the pond for the summer."

London Calling

When I accepted the Morgan Stanley internship, I had no idea that it was one of the few paying positions of all the companies in the program, which was good news for a kid staring at tens of thousands of dollars in college loans. I headed overseas for the summer of 1990, between my junior and senior years.

I was placed in the Operations Control department and was responsible for telling traders about the errors they made in their accounts. My manager was a nice enough guy, an expatriate who seemed to like having someone to talk with about American sports. When it was time for me to return to the States, I asked him for a letter of recommendation. The first one (shown on the next page) was handed to me as a joke. The second one—the real one—provided the key to the vault.

I looked forward to stepping onto the loud and chaotic floor to absorb the energy each day. There was something uniquely powerful about the way the business was transacted. It felt like I was standing at the very center of capitalism and commerce. I lifted weights in college, and I wasn't a small guy, and while that had proved helpful at Harry's, it provided little utility in the high-stakes world of trading. The environment was scary yet exciting, and unlike anything that I had ever experienced.

By the end of the summer, I was physically drained, emotionally spent, intellectually challenged, and completely sold. When I returned to the States, accounting was no longer an option.

I didn't want to crunch the numbers. *I wanted to create them.*

MORGAN STANLEY

MORGAN STANLEY INTERNATIONAL
COLEGRAVE HOUSE
70 BERNERS STREET
LONDON W1P 3AE

19 July 1990

To Whom It May Concern:

Todd Harrison worked in the Operations Control department for Morgan Stanley International, London during the summer of 1990 as a summer intern. I found him to be incredibly lazy, never on time for work - in short, totally useless. He was incompetent to the point that the firm incurred losses of several millions of dollars and were sued by no fewer than 48 of our clients. Everything this boy touched turned to shit! All he ever thought about was getting laid and even attempted to ████ the managing directors daughter. Never in my life have I experienced a person such as this. If you are thinking of employing him in any capacity you should have your head examined!! It will take us years to sort out the problems he caused.
His only good point was that he had excellent drug connections.

Should you need any further information on this lowlife, feel free to contact me as soon as I return from the rest home.

Thank God he's gone.

Respectively yours,

████████████████████

Manager, Operations Control
Morgan Stanley International

TELEPHONE 01 709 3000   FACSIMILE 01 709 4960   TELEX 8812564

REGISTERED IN ENGLAND, NO. 1281413. A SUBSIDIARY OF MORGAN STANLEY GROUP INC   REGISTERED OFFICE: KINGSLEY HOUSE, 1A WIMPOLE STREET, LONDON W1M 7AA

MEMBER OF THE SECURITIES ASSOCIATION AND THE ASSOCIATION OF FUTURES BROKERS AND DEALERS

The Relationship Business

My senior year was supposed to be a final stretch of innocent fun before I embarked on a career path. I had the college experience down and looked forward to my Syracuse finale. While I had one eye on the future, my other body parts were firmly committed to squeezing every ounce of enjoyment from my remaining time in upstate New York.

The weekend after I arrived home from London, I was at my girlfriend's home in New Jersey. It was raining, there wasn't much on television, and we had already eaten, among other things. Bored, I decided to call my aunt, who lived nearby, to see how she was doing. As we caught up, she told me about a friend of hers who worked at Morgan Stanley. "You should give him a ring," she said. "He's a great guy."

I called Chuck Feldman, who I would later learn was a legend on Wall Street. He pioneered the equity derivative business and ran the show at Morgan Stanley; he was the quintessential old-school trader, a guy who worked his way to the top and stayed there. He was, as we used to say in the day, "the man." His high-pitched voice was extremely soft-spoken when we were on the phone. That's the first thing I remember about Chuck, how soft-spoken he was. It would be the last time I ever had that thought.

It was an hour that ultimately handed me the keys to the cash register.

He lived in a neighboring town and invited me to swing by to shake his hand. We met for an hour, took a ride to the supermarket and had a pleasant enough conversation; I remember thinking that he wasn't a large man, but his presence cast a long shadow.

It was an hour that would forever change my professional path.

It was an hour that ultimately handed me the keys to the cash register.

The Fast Track

I was preparing for the annual Zeta Psi toga party at the end of the first semester of my senior year when the phone rang.

"Hey, Todd, it's Chuck. Listen—we have an opening on the desk, and I need to know if you're interested." I was surprised at how noisy the trading room was in the background. His voice was no longer soft.

"Uh, I'm very interested," I said as I held the phone in one hand and a Coor's Light in the other, "but what about school?"

"You can finish up by mail." he shot back, seemingly wanting an immediate answer. He paused to bark an order at someone and then mumbled something I couldn't quite catch. "Let me know if you can start next week!"

It was the shot I had been waiting for, a once-in-a-lifetime opportunity to bypass the rigorous two-year training program at a top-tier firm, which would have spit me back out to get my MBA. It was a chance to sit on the trading desks of one of the best financial institutions in the world.

I spent the next day chasing down my professors, pleading with them to shift my course load so I could immediately start at Morgan and still graduate with my class. One by one, they agreed, and by the next day, I was set. My girlfriend cried in the background as I picked up the phone to deliver the news to Chuck.

"I'll be there Monday morning," I said in the most confident tone I could muster, trying to mask my nervousness. There was silence.

"Hey kid," he finally said, "why don't you finish school and call me when you're done."

I didn't know what that meant—was I getting the job? Did I do something wrong? Did he change his mind? All these thoughts raced through my mind before I realized he already had hung up.

I finished my senior year, occasionally calling Chuck in hopes of staying on his radar. Each time he was cordial, but at no point did he renew his offer. I tried to enjoy the rest of my college experience despite the anxiety that emerged every time one of my classmates landed a job.

I could almost smell the money.

Finally, in the spring of 1991, I got the call: "Come in kid, we'll see what we can do." To this day, I don't know if Chuck's initial offer was a test to see how badly I wanted the position or an impetuous gesture he later second-guessed. It didn't matter; I had my foot in the door and the opportunity to prove myself, much like at Harry's but with entirely more on the line.

The Monday following my graduation, as my friends left to backpack in Europe and I nursed a wicked hangover, I paced the pristine lobby at 1251 Avenue of the Americas.

I could almost smell the money.

4

Let the Games Begin!

I remember my first day on the derivative desk at Morgan Stanley's New York office as if it were yesterday. There I was—6'1", 215 pounds of muscle, straight A's in my back pocket, and so scared that I could barely move. It was precisely where I wanted to be, rubbing elbows with the big hitters who wore Armani suits and had fat wallets. I remember thinking that one day, that would be me; at whatever the cost and no matter the price, *that* was my professional nirvana. There was one problem with my master plan—I was completely and utterly clueless.

They placed me at a turret in the middle of the trading desk, gave me a computer, plugged in two phones, handed me a few pages with trading positions, and told me to pick up the blinking lights and relay messages. It sounded simple enough until a red light—one of hundreds of lines that connected Morgan Stanley to various exchanges, brokers, and offices around the world—began to blink. I raised the phone to my ear.

There was one problem with my master plan—I was completely and utterly clueless.

"Two-and-three-eighths, three-quarters-five-hundred-up!"

Huh?

I stared blankly at the phone grid and tried to comprehend what I was supposed to communicate to the rest of the team. I looked around to see if someone could help me translate the message, but everyone already had phones pressed against their ears.

"Who the fuck took a market from the Amex?"

The words sliced through the room in a high-pitched voice and everyone—I mean everyone—stopped what they were doing. I swallowed hard and slid down in my chair as Chuck screamed at the clerk on the Amex, calling him a liar and threatening to fire everyone in his family.

Thank God I never said a word when I picked up the phone.

Thank God nobody knew it was the kid in the cheap suit who was too afraid to speak.

The Boston Bruin

The Morgan Stanley trading room was a massive labyrinth that occupied the entire floor of 1251 Avenue of the Americas. The equity derivative desk was nestled against the far center window with the listed stock desk, over-the-counter trading, convertible arbitrage desk, and international department strategically situated around it. If trading was the bloodline of Morgan Stanley, options were the heartbeat, and the fervor of each day's flow revolved around our desk.

I noticed that one of the traders on the over-the-counter desk made more noise than the rest. He was the alpha trader—when he laughed, the mood lightened and when he yelled, everyone froze. His name was David Slaine, and he ran OTC trading for Morgan Stanley.

When one of his customers had a trade to make that tied into the order flow on the derivative desk, he negotiated with the options department to set the price. During one of my first days, David was standing behind my chair as he worked an order, and when I turned my head to catch a glance, he looked down and introduced himself.

"You look like you work out," he said in a thick Boston accent. "You should come to the gym with us after the close."

I couldn't relay an order to save my life, I didn't understand most of what was happening in the markets, and I was unaware of the politics that consumed those around me. I did, however, know how to lift weights.

It reminded me of my pledge class in Syracuse after a semester of hell, and it was a feeling that few would understand from the outside looking in.

That afternoon, I joined David and Tommy Carden, a senior trader on the options desk, for a workout near our midtown office. There was camaraderie between them, a bond that was forged through long days in the trenches. They waged a vicious battle every session, but at the end of the day, they were regular guys who spotted each other on the bench and grabbed dinner afterward. It reminded me of my pledge class in Syracuse after a semester of hell, and it was a feeling that few would understand from the outside looking in.

It was very much a fraternity I wanted to join.

Engine Room, More Steam!

It all happened so fast—one moment was I flipping bottles in Syracuse and the next I was on the derivative desk at one of the world's most prestigious financial institutions. I lived in my grandparents' apartment, awoke each morning at the crack of dawn, and was so intimidated when I got to work that I wouldn't even get up to go to the bathroom. I had to earn my stripes all over again in a strange, new world.

I was determined to make up for what I lacked in experience with effort and energy. Unfortunately, despite four years of schooling and the debt to prove it, I didn't have a practical working knowledge of the business. When I had been in school, I asked one of my professors how to better prepare for life as an options trader and he told me to read *The Wall Street Journal* and study a Black-Scholes model, neither of which did much good.

I was overwhelmed by the speed and intensity on the trading floor and attempted to mask my ignorance by keeping my head down and not speaking unless spoken to. I later learned that other traders, many of whom took a more traditional path to get there, thought I was cocky. Some of them worked in the back office or toiled in operations and waited years for their shot to sit where I was. I was oblivious to the competition, animosity, and resentment. I didn't know any better, and I suppose, it was just as well.

Wall Street was an exclusive fraternity, and it was up to me to gain their respect and earn the right to represent Morgan Stanley in the global battle for financial dominance. I pushed myself, picked up more phones, and relayed bigger orders, but the harder I tried, the more mistakes I made, and my self-doubt morphed into a complete lack of confidence. I couldn't seem to grasp the business, but I committed myself to doing whatever it took to lend value to the operation. I was going to do whatever anyone else didn't have the time to do.

During one particularly hectic morning with wild market swings, I offered to grab lunch for Jack Skiba, the second-in-command behind Chuck Feldman. I told him that I made a mean salad and watched closely for a response. He grumbled something and reached for his wallet.

"I got it," I said, slowly reaching toward my empty pocket. "Stop!" he responded, seeing through my obvious gesture.

I must have spent 20 minutes making that salad. The tomatoes and onions were perfectly aligned. Grilled chicken danced across the center. A drizzle of dressing tied a bow around the top. It was a masterpiece, and I was ready to present it.

I dropped the salad on Jack's desk, took my seat next to him, and pretended to focus as he glanced at my work of art. A few hours later, long after he finished eating, he turned to me and said, "Nice salad, kid."

Try not to laugh, but that was my first victory at Morgan Stanley; it was a ray of sunlight during an otherwise trying time. I realized at that moment that Wall Street was a relationship business, and I had suddenly gained sponsorship. All I needed to do was perform.

A Simple Twist of Fate

While I was the second or third person on the trading floor each morning, I was the first person on the derivative desk. It was my responsibility to "write up" Chuck's trading positions and "pare them off" so he could monitor the risk.

Slowly, I began to learn. Long common stock and short call options were a "buy-write." Long calls and short stock were each a "synthetic put." Long put and long stock combined was a "married put." These phrases probably don't mean all that much to you, and, at the time, they didn't mean much to me.

It seemed silly that the world's largest derivative desk had a clueless kid writing up the head trader's risk profile in T-accounts each morning. It's all the more ironic that despite fancy modern-day risk management, that very same derivative machination would eventually implode under its own weight and almost collapse the global capital market construct.

One morning, as I labored through my daily ritual, a blinking light sprung to life. I wasn't supposed to pick up "the Cramer wire" since it was a direct line to a customer. I looked at the clock; it was barely 6:00 a.m. The blinking stopped—I was off the hook...and then it began again, and it didn't stop; I picked up the phone.

"Hello?"

A frenetic voice on the other end of the line didn't seem to notice that it was still dark outside.

"Heeeeeeey, what's going on?"

"This is Todd," I said. "Nobody's here yet."

"You new?" he asked, friendly enough but in a quickened pace. "We haven't met yet. I'm Cramer. Whadaya think here? What's going on overseas? Do you like 'em? So... Whadaya think?"

I looked toward the elevator banks but there weren't any traders around. I swallowed hard and offered an honest take. "I saw better buyers on the desk yesterday. The smarter accounts were buying stocks for a trade."

"So, do you like 'em?" he again asked, this time in a slightly less friendly tone. I didn't miss a beat, "Yeah, I like 'em."

"I like 'em too!" he shot back. Evidently, I had given him the answer he wanted to hear. "I gotta hop—they're gonna rip 'em today. Rip 'em!"

One of the first things my grandfather taught me was that all a man has is his name and his word.

The line went dead while the receiver was still nestled against my ear, and I'll never forget the tension that I felt as the markets opened. I had skin in the game—not money, but my reputation.

One of the first things my grandfather taught me was that all a man has is his name and his word. Both were on the line, and, after the market meandered on both sides of the flat line for the better part of the session, stocks rallied hard into the close and finished near their highs. I was hooked.

Bonus, Baby

Holiday season arrived after I had been there seven months, and it was bonus time at Morgan Stanley. As other traders received word on their multiple six- or seven-figure bonuses, I anxiously awaited my turn. When nobody was left on the desk, Jack called me into the back offices.

When I had started, I was given a base salary of $28,000. I knew Wall Street professionals earned the bulk of their compensation through bonuses, so I wasn't all that concerned. I sat down and smiled; Jack didn't smile back.

"You need to step it up," he told me as the color drained from my face. "If you want to be around next year, you have to find a way to contribute to the bottom line."

I nodded my head in agreement. I knew he was right, but somewhere deep within me, I secretly hoped they would throw me a bone. I quickly discovered nothing came for free, and, as much as I thought that Wall Street was a relationship business, I quickly learned that it was a results-oriented machine.

I committed myself to earn my keep the next 12 months—I wanted to be in that room again and walk out with the big bucks. I continued to be the first person to arrive each day and the last one to leave. I studied books on options pricing and read *The Wall Street Journal* religiously, even if I didn't understand it all. I established a rapport with the floor traders and others on the desk, waiting for lulls in their day to lob an occasional question. In time, I became comfortable with my ability to relay markets to the sales force and take reports on completed transactions.

"General Motors, symbol GM, October 40 calls. 1 1/4- 1/2, 500 up!"

"International Business Machines, symbol IBM, January 20 puts, 2 1/2- 3/4, 250 up!"

"Citigroup, you bought 1000 calls at 2 even. 3/4- 1/4 250 on either side coming out!"

I hadn't made the team, but I was clearly on the field. I knew, however, that spring training would soon come to an end. I needed to break the pattern; I needed to evolve from being that kid who knew the vernacular to the trader who made markets.

When Chuck tossed an odd-lot 1000 share order of Pet Industries on the desk of Harry Silver, the trader to my left, he passed it to me. "Go sell this," he said, quietly so that nobody could hear. It was my first order on Wall Street, and I wasn't going to sell it at market prices. I offered the shares above the market with hopes that someone would pay up.

I picked up the phone and cleared my voice. "Pet Industries, ticker P-E-T. Offer 500 shares at 3/4."

The stock immediately traded lower; not by a lot—perhaps a half point—but it didn't matter. The entire world stopped except for that one order as what would become an all too familiar knot began to tie in my stomach. I never sold a share, and the stock was down a buck and change. A few hours later, Chuck screamed to Harry, "Did I sell my PET?"

Harry knew I hadn't as soon as he saw the look of pure horror on my face. "Just tell him you sold it—I'll take care of it."

The Morgan Stanley derivative desk had hundreds of millions of dollars in exposure at any given time. One thousand shares of Pet was a pimple on an elephant's ass; it didn't matter, and nobody would have known if I "cuffed" the report. For me, however, it was the single biggest moment of my professional life.

My grandfather's advice rang loudly in my ear. All you have is your name and your word. I dropped the ball, but I wasn't about to compromise my integrity. "No," I said carefully. "I didn't sell it."

Harry closed his eyes.

"What the fuck! Jack, fire the fucking kid!" He threw down his pen, kicked his chair from under him, and stormed off the desk, shaking his head in disbelief.

I dropped the ball, but I wasn't about to compromise my integrity.

After the close, Tommy asked me what happened. "I didn't execute the order; Harry told me to tell Chuck that I did, but I don't lie."

It would be two years before Harry said another word to me.

The Great Lawn

While spending a day in Central Park that summer with my golden retriever Jackson, I ran into a friend who was sitting with a group of people, most of whom I didn't know. She asked me to join them, so I sat on the grass and introduced myself to her friends.

One of them was Jeff Berkowitz, who was an analyst at Jim Cramer's hedge fund. Jeff and I immediately connected, not because of where he worked but because of who he was. We related to each other on a variety of levels, from the markets to sports to women. We were both diehard Yankee fans and ardent stock enthusiasts.

After that meeting, we spoke often, shared ideas, and swapped insights. He was a sharp guy, and I was eager to learn as much as I could from him. His fundamental analysis differed from the technical approach that we employed on the Morgan Stanley derivative desk. I would eventually learn that four primary metrics defined the price action of a stock, or a market of stocks: fundamental analysis, technical analysis, structural influences, and market psychology.

I began to assimilate those four metrics as legs under the trading table, and when they were sturdy in alignment, the odds of profitability skewed heavily in my favor. It was an approach that I utilized for the rest of my career, and it was one that worked incredibly well—most of the time.

5

War Stories

If I were to pick a word that characterized 1992, it would be survival. I didn't scale the learning curve as quickly as I would have liked, but I had a seat at the table and that had to mean something.

At Morgan Stanley, we were measured by four criteria: personal performance, departmental performance, divisional performance, and overall firm performance. If any of those elements were sub-par, it would invariably trickle down; Wall Street firms, despite their outsized pay packages, had an uncanny knack of dangling a bigger and better carrot in front of their people.

With the recession of 1989–1991 fading in the rearview mirror, the mood on our desk was optimistic. We had a monster year, and I had made considerable progress forging professional inroads and networking with customers. When the holiday season arrived, I confidently walked into the back office. Jack was again waiting for me.

"You know," he began, "Wall Street isn't for everyone. You're a good kid and people like you, but this may not be the business for you." He paused, choosing his words carefully. "You need to think—really think—if this is something you want to pursue. If it is, you've got to show us something and it has to be soon."

I tried to mask my disappointment while at the same time appear stoic.

"I'm not going to let you down," I said, never losing eye contact. "This is where I belong, Jack. I'm not going to let you down. I'm not going to let myself down." I waited, perhaps hoping he would say something, but he didn't. I again spoke, this time with purpose. "I give you my word."

He nodded to me and gestured toward the door, confirming what I already knew. For the second straight year, my total annualized compensation at one of the world's most powerful financial institutions was a grand total of $28,000.

Settling Down and Settling In

If 1991 was the year of the salad and 1992 was my wake-up call, 1993 was when I finally found some rhythm. In addition to taking reports and relaying markets, I traded orders given to our desk by the sales force on behalf of our clients. The process was simple: If a customer wanted to buy or sell something, I executed the order with a third-party and relayed the "fill" to the salesperson who in turn, gave a report to the client. That was called *agency business*, and it was usually a six-to-eight minute process. If the marketplace didn't provide liquidity at the right price, Morgan Stanley stepped in and took the other side of the trade. That was called *customer facilitation*.

The Morgan Stanley derivative portfolio was comprised of the aggregate positions created as a function of customer facilitation. The risk profile was broken down into several "books" and separated by industry. Jack traded the industrials, drugs, and airlines. Tommy Carden and Mark Neuberger traded technology. Various other traders, about ten in total, covered the other sectors. Two industries that weren't covered on the desk were the financials and biotechnology. We didn't have positions in those stocks, and I fielded that order flow and executed it on an agency basis, which is to say that I didn't position the risk on behalf of the firm.

One afternoon, several months into 1993, the floor "fell down" on an order; they didn't stand up to what was originally communicated and reflected to the customer. I alerted Tommy, and he told me to "put the customer up." In other words, he told me to position the risk.

I wouldn't say that I had cracked the code, but at least I knew where to look for the combination.

I told my broker on the floor to take the other side of the trade and listened as he slapped it on the tape. Once I got the report, our sales representative told the customer that he was "done" on his order. Tommy told me to watch the position, which effectively meant that I had my first—albeit meager—trading position at Morgan Stanley. When I traded out of it for a profit, he gave me the green light to facilitate another order. That, too, was traded for a profit.

It wasn't much risk—50 and 100 lot orders, which, given options have a multiplier of 100, equated to 5,000 or 10,000 shares of stock, but I traded them with discipline. As the year progressed, the cumulative profits I generated for the firm grew in kind. I worked harder than I ever had before, bouncing out of bed at 5:00 a.m. each day and racing across town to my office. I wouldn't say that I had cracked the code, but at least I knew where to look for the combination.

When 1993 came to a close, I again sat with Jack in the back room. This time he had a smile on his face as he told me my total compensation rose to $75,000. At 24 years old, I had made more money than I knew what to do with.

Changes in Latitude, Changes in Attitude

While there was still much to learn, I had secured my spot on the desk. I didn't produce the revenue the other traders did, but I consistently contributed to the bottom line and did what I could to further our collective mission. I still made Jack salads every day, and I was more than happy to do so.

David Slaine, "Slaino," was my big brother, Jack my father figure, and Tommy took me under his wing with increased frequency, which included taking me to see a number of Grateful Dead shows. I can't tell you exactly how many times he and I left on the closing bell and swapped our ties for tie-dyes, but it happened on multiple occasions for a number of years. The rest of the department warmed up as well and seemed to enjoy the stories I shared on Monday mornings following a weekend full of fun. I was young then and didn't have the responsibility of a family or mortgage payments. My priorities were making money and getting laid, in that order.

There were several regime changes while I was in the derivatives department. Chuck retired after my third year and handed the leadership baton to a younger, more quantitative risk manager. I didn't understand the politics behind that decision, but it didn't concern me. While Chuck gave me my shot and I remain grateful to this day, I was more concerned with self-preservation and the next rung on the money ladder.

My compensation paled in comparison to the other traders and perhaps that's why I felt somewhat secure. In terms of bang for the buck, I was the best deal on the desk.

Every day was like an ever-changing jigsaw puzzle that fit together to form a bottom line shaped by world events and investor perception.

With time and experience, my performance gained steam, and I produced in a more meaningful manner. Every day was like an ever-changing jigsaw puzzle that fit together to form a bottom line shaped by world events and investor perception. When a customer traded one of my "names," the order was dropped directly on my desk. I no longer had to check with Jack or Tommy; I had discretion to determine what I wanted to position on behalf of the firm and what I wanted to pass to the street. Autonomy is the ultimate sign of respect on Wall Street, and once that arrived the money wasn't far behind.

At the end of 1994, management pulled me in back and informed me my total compensation was $150,000. Drinks were on me.

The Moment of Truth

Things had really started to come together. I built the bank's pad into one of the biggest on the Street, and word quickly spread about the kid from Morgan with steely nerves and a penchant for making aggressive markets. If someone had something to do in the banking sector, I was the call. I traded huge positions, took care of my customers, and plunked money into Mother Morgan's till on a consistent basis.

Keefe Bruyette was the biggest player in the financial sector and the crown jewel of the customer base that trafficked in banking stocks. I worked hard to impress their head trader and before long, secured a nice chunk of their order flow. Nationsbank, Chemical Bank, Chase Manhattan Bank—you name it, we traded it. I was only 26 years old, and I had already established myself as a customer-friendly producer. If you wanted to trade a bank, you came to Morgan and knew you would get taken care of.

The First Interstate position began like any other. The stock was trading around $70 when Keefe's head trader asked Kim Dispigna, his Morgan Stanley institutional salesperson, for a market in the Jan par leaps (January 100 call options that gave the owner the right, but not the obligation, to buy First Interstate at $70 until the third Friday of the following January). I checked the floor market and found that the options were three dollars wide and 50 up, meaning the customer could buy or sell 50 contracts (5,000 shares of common stock) on either side of an illiquid market.

"What odd-lots," I seethed to myself as I tightened the market and increased the size tenfold, meaning that I would allow the customer the option to buy or sell 500 options—the equivalent of 50,000 shares of stock—at a better price than the floor market. "Whatever he needs," I told Kim. "Just get the order."

Keefe took me on my offer, and then continued to buy upside exposure over the course of a few days. Before long, we had both accumulated a large position; I was short the call options (which gave my customer the right to purchase stock), and I had bought common stock and other call options to hedge that risk. The customer became increasingly aggressive, wanting to buy more and more call options, and I had trouble keeping up. Other traders on the floor wouldn't sell any more calls, and I was the only source of liquidity.

Finally, after several weeks of that daily dance, the customer asked what the position limit was.

"8,500 contracts," I replied. "That's as many contracts as he's allowed to buy, according to the exchange." We were almost there; 8,500 call options gave the customer the right, but not the obligation, to purchase 850,000 shares of common stock at the strike price, which was $70, until they expired the following January. Given the stock was trading well above $100, those calls, some $30 "in the money," might as well have been straight stock.

To say that I was involved in First Interstate is like saying that Google is involved in the Internet. If anyone on Wall Street had something to do in the name, they knew Morgan Stanley was the call. I had a massive position—short the long-term calls to my customer and long everything under the sun, including near-term calls and a boatload of stock, against them. I assumed the customer knew something—there was persistent chatter in the marketplace that First Interstate was a takeover candidate—and I intended to go along for the ride.

I traded that monster for months. When I liked the broader market, I pressed my upside bet and bought more stock against my position; at times, I carried upward of 150,000 shares of net long exposure in the position, which was sizable given the underlying value of the stock. When I turned cautious on the market, I shorted other banks against my position, but I never wavered from carrying a considerable upside bet in First Interstate.

Everyone in the room knew the story, and I was sitting on top of The Takeover Express, waiting for it to pull into the Promised Land. The position carried with it incredible stress, but I had a razor sharp edge and the support of management, who had signed off on the risk. I was in the proverbial zone.

Cuts Like a Knife

It was a slow afternoon when Kim's voice sliced through the quiet room.

"How ya makin' Letter I?"

I assumed she was kidding, as she was apt to do. For all the pressure we dealt with each day, for the billions of dollars in risk on our balance sheet at any given time, there was a collegiate atmosphere on the trading floor. That too would change, as would the mainstream perception of the industry.

I looked at my screen, not bothering to call my floor broker to see what the market was. "There's 50 offered at 23 1/2, I'll make it 500 (50,000 shares of stock). Whadaya wanna do?" I said, calling her bluff.

"He needs a two-sided market," she shot back, looking for a bid to see where her customer could sell his call options; the look on her face told me she wasn't joking.

"Really?"

"Yeah."

I measured her; I was no longer smiling. "21 1/2-23 1/2 500 up," I offered with a slight crack in my voice.

"He'll sell ya 500 at 1/2, and he's got more behind it."

I'm not sure I breathed for the next several minutes. I slapped 500 contracts on the tape and called my floor broker to sell some of my underlying exposure. Unfortunately, every option trader on the floor knew the size of my customer's position, and the stock was a dollar lower before I could blink. The closing bell was an hour away, and an uneventful session suddenly became the most important day of my career.

"Keep reflecting bids," Kim said. "I think he wants to get done today."

I needed to make sales to adjust my exposure and asked Kim to ask Keefe if I could "get in shape." That's how business was done; I took risk on behalf of my customer to facilitate his order flow, and with no "working order" in hand, I could sell as much stock as I wanted. I assumed that he wanted to unload the rest of his exposure, and I began to sell stock in anticipation of that trade. If he was going to sell 8,000 call options—which represented 800,000 shares—I knew I would have to buy most of them.

With 15 minutes left in the session, after a furious series of transactions, I yelled, "Figure bid for 8,000!"

I needed Keefe to sell me the rest of his position so I could unwind the remainder of my risk. I watched Kim as she spoke to their head trader, clenching my jaw as I pressed the phone tightly against my ear. My floor broker was at the ready; the order began to form at my lips.

"*Great* bid," she said. "He's gonna hold tight and finish up in the morning."

Sleepless in Manhattan

I was the first person on the trading floor the next day for no other reason than I hadn't been able to sleep. At 6:00 a.m., the bank trader from the listed stock desk walked over with a big grin on his face and said, "You're still involved in Letter I, right?"

"Yeah...?"

"You're...you're still long it, right? Please tell me you're still long it?"

My mouth opened but nothing came out, and he turned and walked away without saying a word. I grabbed the *Journal*, headed to the men's room and stepped into the far stall. Three minutes later, the entire trading floor erupted with a boisterous cheer. I'm not sure how long I sat there but it didn't matter. I desperately wanted to stay. My eyes were glued to the paper, but I couldn't tell you a thing that it said.

Shit.

I was screwed—massively, totally, and completely screwed.

I took several deep, labored breaths, left the *Journal* on the floor and stepped out of the bathroom. You would have thought that I hit a walk-off homerun in the bottom of the ninth inning and my teammates were surrounding home plate at Yankee Stadium. Salesmen patted me on the back, traders gave me the thumbs up, and friends from around the Street left messages to congratulate me. The head of my department walked up with a sparkle in his eye and almost hugged me.

"Way to go, Toddo! Way to stick it out!"

There was only one problem; after selling the majority of my stock in anticipation of buying back the remaining 8,000 calls from the customer, I was short—very short—betting the stock would decline and I would be able to cover the rest of my position for a profit. I was screwed—massively, totally, and completely screwed. The stock was trading 35 points higher, and what would have been a sizable seven-figure win quickly morphed into a multiple-seven figure loss.

Wells Fargo was in talks with First Interstate and the deal evidently fell apart, which may have been the reason Keefe tried to sell his position. I didn't know and it didn't matter; Wells Fargo made a hostile bid, which at the time was unheard of in the banking sector, and the stock was on a moon shot. To make matters worse, Morgan Stanley was the banker on the deal, and I was restricted from trading either stock. My position was taken from me on the opening print; not only was I screwed—I didn't have the opportunity to unscrew myself.

I didn't move from my seat all day. I didn't go to the bathroom. I didn't eat lunch. I didn't make outgoing calls. I didn't do anything but stare at the flickering "I" that continued to wink and blink and taunt me. I was so flummoxed that when a salesman gave me an order in First Interstate—I was allowed to execute, I just couldn't position—I made a $100,000 error that the firm had to eat. It was a disaster spiraling out of control, and somewhere deep within me, I remember feeling a peculiar twinge, like I had somehow snuck into Morgan Stanley and reality finally caught up to me.

Someone had once told me that on Wall Street, you're only as good as your last trade. I assumed that spoke to the general direction of performance, not the literal interpretation that suddenly sank in.

Around 7:00 p.m., Ralph Reynolds, the head of my department, called me into his office. Here we go, I thought, the end of my world as I knew it. Someone had once told me that on Wall Street, you're only as good as your last trade. I assumed that spoke to the general direction of performance, not the literal interpretation that suddenly sank in.

I was so close to the cash register, yet after a single trade, my career was over. I would have banked millions of dollars if the deal was announced a day earlier. Instead, after what may have been an eight-figure overnight swing, I was going to be a sacrificial lamb. My self-esteem was shattered as I prepared myself for the inevitable news.

I explained the sequence of events to Ralph as he stared deep into my eyes. My trading account was still substantially higher for the year—despite the loss, I was firmly in the black—but I was certain it wouldn't matter. He measured me as if he was judging my soul, and after a long pause, he spoke.

"Go home, get some rest, and come ready to play tomorrow."

The immense pressure, the monstrous swings, the incredible stakes, the thin line between success and failure.... Welcome to Wall Street, I thought to myself; welcome to the machine.

He wasn't happy about the loss, but he wasn't going to spike my career over it. The mechanics of my swing, he decided, outweighed the results of that particular at-bat. It's a hell of a thing to have your livelihood hang in the balance of one man's mood.

I walked out of his office, took the elevator downstairs, exited Morgan Stanley's corporate headquarters, and turned the corner. There, as I leaned against the building across the street, surrounded by the denizens of tourists in Times Square who made their way to the theater, I began to laugh. Within a few seconds, tears streamed down the sides of my cheeks.

The immense pressure, the monstrous swings, the incredible stakes, the thin line between success and failure....

Welcome to Wall Street, I thought to myself; welcome to the machine.

6

An Officer and a Gentleman

Following the Letter I fiasco, management watched the way I traded like a baseball manager watches a slugger after he's been hit in the head by a fastball. It took some time for me to regain my confidence, but I again found my stroke after connecting on a few solid trades.

I never understood if ADD people made good traders or if the constant assimilation of a sensory overload environment made traders ADD. Either way, Letter I stopped taunting me, and life again assumed a sense of normalcy. That was the way the business worked: make money and all was forgiven.

There used to be an ingrained ethos on Wall Street. I'm not talking about the country club mindset or the opaque engineering that would ultimately befall the industry; I'm referring to the day-to-day operations and the manner in which business was transacted. The phone lines weren't taped when I first started at Morgan Stanley. Back then, it was just like Ruby said: All you had was your name and your word.

"The main thing about money, Bud, is that it makes you do things you don't want to do."

To quote Lou Manheim, "The main thing about money, Bud, is that it makes you do things you don't want to do." The modern-day financial crisis has shed light on the ramifications of the bad behavior that brought the cumulative imbalances to bear. While the spectrum of culpability extended from overleveraged consumers to the institutions that financially engineered the markets to policymakers that were complicit by acceptance, Wall Street acted as the enabler; in the end, they should have known better.

As I traversed my newfound profession in the early '90s, however, I believed in what I did. In my mind, I was greasing the wheels of capitalism and performing a critical function that facilitated free markets. The disparity in compensation between a trader and, say, a teacher was—and remains—unacceptable. In my mid-twenties, I had never stopped to think about that, or the eventual ramifications of the largesse that was evolving. Once I tasted big money, I was addicted to swallowing more and when bonus season arrived at the end of the year, my compensation again doubled to $300,000. I was also promoted, becoming one of the youngest vice-presidents in the firm at the age of 26.

I couldn't help notice the symmetry. At age 13, I was standing behind a counter serving bagels to affluent classmates from the other side of town. Thirteen years later, I could afford to buy the bagel store.

I couldn't help notice the symmetry. At age 13, I was standing behind a counter serving bagels to affluent classmates from the other side of town. Thirteen years later, I could afford to buy the bagel store.

Todd A. Harrison, Vice-President, Global Equity Derivatives, Morgan Stanley.

My business card became my favorite possession. That was how I was programmed—money and status defined my level of success. I didn't believe that I was arrogant or cocky, but in hindsight, my sensibilities were surely skewed.

I was consumed by the material possessions and conspicuous consumption that surrounded me, and did the type of things you might expect from a twenty-something who made a lot of money. I summered in the Hamptons, treated myself to a few Porsches, and migrated from one girlfriend to the next, keeping an eye out for a wife but not looking particularly hard. My grandmother often told me, "You won't catch a clean fish in dirty waters." But I didn't listen. To be honest, I didn't care; I was too busy having fun to worry about finding happiness.

Inside the office, I noticed a subtle shift in the general perception. Older salesmen and traders who were passed over for promotion adopted a different attitude. The mornings I rumbled in with a hangover were no longer considered cute or funny. I was an officer of the firm who took home a larger slice of the bonus pie; it was suddenly considered unprofessional, and resentment began to percolate.

That was my first real taste of Morgan Stanley politics; the nasty maneuvering that exists in most large organizations. I knew that if I continued to produce, the critics would be silenced. My innocence was gone, but it was replaced with power, and that was a trade I was willing to make.

After years of reaching for the brass ring, my grasp around it had firmed and I liked the way it felt. I upgraded my wardrobe, dined at the finest restaurants, paid back my college loans, and sent my family on fancy vacations. Life was good, or so I thought, as I had the types of things I was conditioned to aspire to.

Perhaps I was blinded by the dollar signs, but it didn't register. As 1996 rolled through, I was certain that my best days were directly ahead.

Welcome to the Jungle

As I climbed the Morgan Stanley ranks, I took tremendous pride in what I did and how I did it. The equity floor was a financial juggernaut, and the derivative desk was at the center of it all. We all wore MORGAN across our chest like a badge of honor. It was us against Goldman Sachs, the two titans on the Street in a rivalry that made the Yanks and Red Sox look like high school sweethearts.

In the mid-nineties, "off-board" derivatives were created, and that opened the door to an entirely new revenue stream for Wall Street firms. Years earlier, when stocks and bonds became too "traditional," options and futures were created as vehicles of trade. Eventually, exotic swaps and other instruments were introduced as the next tier of professional products.

Morgan Stanley was one of the first firms to price over-the-counter derivative products, and we would win business by 30, 40, or 50 volatility points (a subjective assignment in the valuation model). Customers "collared" their stock (bought puts and sold calls to lock in a price level) and laid off the risk without any footprints on an exchange; we gladly facilitated the orders, and we made a lot of money doing it.

Technology companies awoke to write "naked off-board puts" in lieu of stock buy-backs. If the short put options they wrote (which gave the company the right to buy their stock at a particular strike price) were exercised, the cost basis was cheaper than it would have been to buy stock in the open market. If not, the premium expired worthless, and the income slipped through a tax-free loophole.

Microsoft did it. So did Dell. Intel too. In time, as other firms entered the marketplace, increasingly more products were created, one more complex than the next. Wall Street had an uncanny ability to continually recreate and repackage risk, and sell that risk to customer segments that were eager to differentiate returns.

While my career path was on solid footing, I saw bad things happen to good people during the regime changes. The steady stalwarts—the guys who came to work and did their job each day—were passed over for promotion in favor of the politically savvy professionals who knew how to play the game. I learned a lot during those years, particularly when I was perceived as a threat to the establishment. That never made much sense to me, since I was a producer on the desk and an ambassador of our institution.

I was asked to recruit on behalf of the firm. They sent me to UCLA and North Carolina, put me up in swanky hotels, and told me to interview college coeds to weed out the best in breed for the privilege to enter our training program. Morgan's blue blood flowed through my veins, and I did what I could to further our cause. I was a lifer, or so I thought at the time. In hindsight, I was naïve.

Agendas abound when money's around, and they're not always consistent with the best interests of the corporate mandate. I never kissed ass or sucked up, and that didn't sit well with Mark Neuberger, the man who deftly navigated the changing landscape to become the managing director of the options department in 1996.

After the second management shakeup of my tenure at Morgan Stanley, Mark was slated to run the equity derivative trading operation. He stepped over a lot of good people to get there, including Jack Skiba, and unfortunately, his plans didn't include an up-and-comer with plans of his own.

When several high profile traders defected to other firms, Mark was thrown into the role and eager to put his thumbprint on the operation. He assumed trading ownership of the most active tech stocks such as Dell, Intel, Microsoft, and Cisco—the positions with massive over-the-counter derivative positions and, by extension, the largest P&L (profit and loss).

His strategy was simple: He wanted to trade the most liquid names trafficked by the largest customers and leave the tougher trades for others to navigate. There were times when one of our customers entered an order in an illiquid stock, and Mark instructed me to facilitate the transaction.

"One firm-firm," he said as he passed the risk, knowing that my P&L would bear the brunt of the damage. It was a delicate balance. To get the "easy" trades, we needed to absorb the more difficult risk, but his agenda was clear, even to me. Sometimes I facilitated the orders, and other times I refused. One time, when I took down a sizable chunk of call options that immediately moved against me for a six-figure loss, he laughed and said, "There it goes!"

After a few months of friction, I was summoned to the human resources department high atop our new tower at 1585 Broadway. When I walked into the conference room, several people were seated around a large oak table. Mark Neuberger sat at the far end.

I was informed that I was being put on probation for conduct unbecoming a Morgan Stanley professional. I studied the faces in the room, and when my eyes met Mark and he looked down at the table, I knew precisely what was happening. I had heard about ambushes like that, but I hadn't seen it coming. A few months later, when I was handed my annual review, there, on a single piece of paper, it said that the other desk heads—the men who ran the listed and over-the-counter operations—didn't trust me.

Odd, I thought. Jon Olesky, the managing director of the listed stock desk, was in charge of recruiting and personally picked me to represent the firm on the trips to North Carolina and UCLA. David Slaine, who ran the OTC desk, was my big brother in the firm and one of my closest friends. It was a power struggle pure and simple, and I interpreted this to mean that Mark didn't want me around to challenge his authority.

I protested to Tom Clark, who was one wrung on the management ladder above Mark, and was told that I shouldn't rock the boat. The firm had just sorted through a major shakeup and apparently, there was no room for controversy. He asked me to sign my review, as all employees were required to do. He wanted me to take one for the team. I was upset but didn't want to leave the only firm I had ever worked for.

I didn't want to leave my brothers.

I didn't want to leave the cash register.

The Good Ship

Slaino didn't like what he was seeing; he knew that I was being sandbagged, but since he headed a different department—and given the politics surrounding the defections—his protests fell on deaf ears. I refused to sign the review. I knew that as soon as I put pen to paper, my days at Mother Morgan would be numbered. Seven years, I thought to myself. I wasn't going out like that.

A few months earlier, Raj Rajratanam and Gary Rosenbach, former partners at Needham & Company, had created a powerful new hedge fund. The Galleon Group opened for business with roughly $500 million under management, and they were the talk of the town. Slaino and Gary were friendly after spending years on the Street together, and David made the introduction. Gary was likeable enough when we first spoke and soon thereafter, I began to facilitate some of his options trades. The more money we made together, the more frequent the conversations became and the more I began to think about a new and different career path.

I didn't want to leave Morgan, but I was fighting a losing battle. My relationship with Neuberger had deteriorated to a nonconversational place, and as he was my direct boss, I knew that he held the keys to my future. Every few days, Tom Clark called me into his office and asked me to sign the review, and each time I declined. I couldn't put it off forever.

With David's endorsement, I began having conversations with Galleon about moving over to their shop. They didn't have a derivative specialist in house, and it felt like a natural fit. As pressure continued to build inside Morgan Stanley, I found myself delving deeper into the opportunity with increased frequency. I didn't know much about hedge funds other than they were the customers and the potential existed to make a lot—and I mean a lot—of money.

After several meetings, we agreed that I would join The Galleon Group as the managing director of derivatives. I would receive a token salary, help shape the derivative exposure for the main fund, and derive the bulk of my compensation from a smaller portfolio that I would oversee.

I walked into Tom Clark's office and shut the door behind me. I expressed my reservations about the falsities contained in the review, and he assured me that I would be taken care of.

"Will I really be taken care of?" I asked.

"You have my word," he said, pushing the document in front of me as he uncapped his pen.

I signed the review, putting my better judgment aside, and when bonus time arrived, I was paid $500,000. I thanked management and waited patiently for the check to clear. Once it did, I walked into Tom's office and tendered my resignation.

They were stuck—not only had they just paid half a million dollars to a departing trader, I was leaving to work for one of the biggest new hedge funds on the Street, which immediately made them one of Morgan Stanley's prized targets.

It was as if a magical money tree blossomed overhead and all I had to do was reach higher if I wanted—or needed—more.

Vikram Pandit, who would later become CEO of Citigroup, ran the Morgan Stanley equity division at the time and called me to his office to offer his congratulations. He said if there was anything I needed to please let him know. I didn't even know that he knew my name; it was certainly the first time he expressed an interest in my well-being.

I gathered my belongings and said good-bye to the only professional family I ever knew. I felt like I out-traded the best desk on Wall Street; the power shoe was on the other foot, and I liked the way it fit.

I flew to Florida to surprise my grandparents and took them to the Lexus dealership, where I told them to pick out the car of their dreams. Ruby had always wanted a Lexus, and the look on his face was priceless; that type of story gets a lot of mileage in Boca Raton. I treated myself to a few watches; when I couldn't decide between three high-end brands, I bought one of each. I ran around New York City and the Hamptons with a large group of friends and footed the bills for everyone involved. Travel was first class, and the hotels were the best in breed; I even qualified for one of those snazzy American Express black cards, which actually meant something to me at the time.

It was as if a magical money tree blossomed overhead and all I had to do was reach higher if I wanted—or needed—more.

7

Trading Places

I would love to say it was easy sailing as I reached for the rudder at The Galleon Group. The truth is that I navigated directly into a perfect storm.

A financial contagion began brewing after Thailand cut the peg between the Thai baht and the US dollar. I had witnessed similar situations on a smaller scale, such as the Orange County derivative scare at the end of 1994, but that was the first such scare that migrated worldwide. As we would experience years later a few times over, it would not be the last—some would argue it was only the beginning.

I was unaware that a butterfly flapping its wings in Asia could create a tsunami on East 57th Street in New York City.

I wasn't thinking about the Thai baht, nor was I focused on a hedge fund in Connecticut called Long Term Capital Management. I was unaware that a butterfly flapping its wings in Asia could create a tsunami on East 57th Street in New York City. I managed the derivative exposure for the main Galleon portfolio and traded my smaller book. As I had never experienced a losing year, I felt impervious as I began the new chapter of my trading career. I would soon learn that the facilitation skills I practiced at Morgan Stanley weren't helpful on the buy-side, where you eat what you kill.

I enjoyed life as a customer; Morgan Stanley, Goldman Sachs, First Boston, Deutsche Bank, and other top-tier firms vied for our business, and their effort assumed many forms, including idea generation, capital commitment, expensive dinners, late nights at strip clubs, and eventually, lavish trips to the Super Bowl. Galleon's assets under management ballooned to billions of dollars, and there was a lot of money being tossed around. Everyone on the Street wanted a slice of that pie.

Brokers stumbled over each other to make a positive impression. Yankee tickets weren't enough; they had to be box seats. Dinner? You name it; anywhere, any time. Can't get a ticket to a concert? Not a problem; someone always had a connection to the front row.

Those were the perks, but the other side wasn't as pleasant. I was surrounded by seasoned professionals, but I struggled with the new process. I no longer had customer order flow to lean against or a well-heeled franchise to tap into. It was a completely different dynamic, and one for which I was entirely unprepared.

There were about eight of us sitting in the main room. Raj sat in an office behind a glass partition within shouting distance from Gary, who ran the trading operation and executed orders on his behalf, as well as his own trades. There were five partners in total and a handful of traders, but I was the only trader with an options background, and I viewed that as my meal ticket within the organization.

I toggled between my two roles, focusing primarily on the derivative portfolio for the flagship fund. Gary, Raj, and the other partners assimilated information at a furious pace and asked me to leverage their ideas through the options market for incremental performance. I would ask, "What's your price target and time horizon?" and suggested strategies that maximized reward relative to the assumed risk.

We didn't just trade calls and puts; we crafted complex options strategies such as butterfly spreads and strangles that optimized volatility and captured catalysts.

The more time I spent on the main fund derivative exposure, the less I focused on trading my own account, which was a decision that I came to regret. While there was tangible value to the speculative bets and hedging strategies I implemented, the losses in my personal portfolio piled up as the financial contagion spread. All of a sudden, my job security was in the hands of a select few whom I barely knew. There would be no bonus—in fact, I was told that I was lucky to have a job.

Reality Check

It was Memorial Day 1998 and despite my struggles at Galleon, I was still committed to having fun when I wasn't trying to make money. I didn't need a car in NYC, but when the summer rolled around, I wanted transportation to and from my summer rental in the Hamptons. A blue Porsche convertible seemed like a fitting ride given my professional trajectory.

When I arrived in Southampton the first night of the summer, I ducked into a nightclub called The Tavern. I knew the folks who ran the joint and didn't make eye contact with the hoards of people waiting on line as the bouncer ushered me past the crowd. I didn't mean any disrespect, but I'm certain it was interpreted as such.

While standing at the inside bar, I felt a "flick" against the back of my right ear and spun around to find one of my closest friends, Joel Pollack, standing there with a goofy grin on his face. Joel and I had met years earlier when we were neighbors in New York City, and we eventually ran a share house in Fire Island before switching to the more upscale Hampton scene. He was what my grandfather called "one of us," a salt of the earth guy who genuinely cared about everyone and tried to do the right thing.

The first thing Joel said to me was, "Did you get the car?" That was his way, always inquiring about others and genuinely interested in the response. We had had long conversations during the weekday nights when we walked our dogs together. He knew about the Morgan drama, and just about everything else in my life.

"Yes," I answered. "It's parked right across the street in front of the pizza shop." He asked to see the car, but I didn't want to walk back outside. "I'll show it to you later," I said, before losing myself in a conversation with a pretty brunette. It was the start of summer and life was good. There was work to be done; there was fun to be had.

When I left the bar a few hours later, there were police cars and fire engines for as far as the eye could see. "Great," I thought to myself, "a sobriety checkpoint." I wasn't drunk, but I had had a couple of drinks; I wanted to get to my rental, where my friends were waiting to celebrate the beginning of summer. As I pulled out of the parking lot, I asked one of the police officers what happened. "Someone got killed," he said. "Happy Memorial Day."

I spent the next day doing the Hampton scene, the "see and be seen" thing. It wasn't until late Sunday when a friend handed me his phone and a voice on the other end said, "Hey man, I'm sorry about Joel" when I realized what had happened.

One week after his 34th birthday, Joel Pollack was dead. I later learned that a drunk driver struck him as he stood on the side of the road, directly in front of where my new car was parked. There was no way to know if he ventured across the street to see the car or if it was simply a coincidence. All I knew is that one of my "brothers" was gone, and I learned a valuable lesson.

There's loss, and there's loss. While Joel was the first of my friends to be taken before his time, he unfortunately would not be the last.

The Beginning of the Bubble

As the world digested the Asian Contagion, former Federal Reserve Chairman Alan Greenspan introduced historic fiscal and monetary stimuli. That set in motion a series of decisions that planted the seeds of the dot.com bubble and would eventually evolve into a multitude of booms and busts the following decade.

David Slaine resigned from Morgan Stanley and joined Galleon as a partner in 1998, and we sat next to each other as Galleon became one of the most powerful funds on Wall Street. I wasn't privy to the information that flowed through the phone lines, but I saw the positions as they were initiated and had the opportunity to tag along if I chose to do so.

Following the script I wrote at Morgan and Harry's before that, I did whatever I could to add value. This time, however, it didn't take the form of a salad—I had experience and a skill-set, and resolved myself to be a productive part of the money-making machine.

I wasn't a partner, which was a fact that I was reminded of often. In one of our morning meetings, I communicated that Russia was imploding—it had caught the "financial flu" from Thailand—and warned that it could infect US financial markets, a thought initially dismissed by the partners. When I pressed the issue, citing the derivative machination that tied the world together, urging them to pay attention to the systemic risks, I was verbally undressed in front of the entire firm. A few days later, stateside markets were consumed by the contagion, and stocks cascaded lower.

Applied Materials, a semiconductor capital equipment company that was one of Raj's favorite stocks at the time—and one I had a position in—melted lower along with the rest of the market. It was a stunning experience, billions of dollars in market value evaporated, vanishing into thin air. It was an expensive lesson as well, as unforeseen forces overwhelmed my stylistic approach to risk management.

All of a sudden, fundamentals and technical analysis didn't matter. Supply overwhelmed anything that got in its way, including our Applied Materials position.

A decade later, the imbalances, cumulative still, would challenge the very existence of free market capitalism, but nobody cared at the time—investors around the world were too busy enjoying the feast before the famine.

After the downdraft—and after I took sizable losses in my trading portfolio—the market rallied in response to a coordinated agenda by central banks around the world as they lowered rates and increased the money supply. Alan Greenspan was lauded as the best Federal Reserve Chairman of all time, although history would teach us that risk wasn't destroyed, it simply changed shape and was pushed out on the time continuum. A decade later, the imbalances, cumulative still, would challenge the very existence of free market capitalism, but nobody cared at the time—investors around the world were too busy enjoying the feast before the famine.

Back to Life, Back in Reality

The capital base and information flow in that small room on East 57th Street was matched only by the size of the egos. They profited in good times and bad, coining money as I crafted derivative strategies that leveraged their ideas and information. I continued to focus the majority of my attention on the main fund, certain that it was my pathway to bigger and better things, perhaps all the way to a vaunted partnership. I knew that was where the big money was—tens if not hundreds of millions of dollars. As 1998 drew to a close, I was finally going to cash in.

If you told me while I was growing up that I would make multiple six-figures in my twenties, I would have been thrilled, but my sights were set on a bigger benchmark. I wanted to be a millionaire by the time I was 30.

Nothing else mattered: My self-worth was a function of my net worth. There were then six partners at Galleon, including David, and there was more than enough money to go around. I knew how much was up for grabs—more wealth than you can possibly imagine—and I did the math in my head. I could smell it—extreme affluence was right around the corner.

I sat down with Gary, exchanged a few pleasantries and awaited communication of my bonus. The terms of my employment were very clear, he explained. While the partners appreciated the work I did managing the derivative risk for the flagship fund—billions of dollars worth of risk—my compensation was based on the performance of my smaller trading account. That was the deal we agreed to, he said, and I should have been thankful to see the partner's order flow, so I could tag along and personally profit.

For the second year in the row, I would receive no bonus.

Green with Envy

I'm not proud to admit this, but I began to covet while I worked at Galleon. The partners made insane money, the type of money superstar athletes and famous actors wouldn't see in a lifetime. They were taking it home each year, facilitating lavish lifestyles with enormous homes, expansive ranches, private jets, and garages full of expensive cars. Money is intoxicating when you're that age, and $500,000 suddenly seemed like a very small amount of money. I had entered the world of the mega-millionaires, rainmakers that set the new standard on the Street. I set my sights at joining the ranks of the Wall Street elite.

The policies introduced by Alan Greenspan kicked in and the stock market climbed the front end of the technology bubble. Fortunes were made on a daily basis as IPOs climbed hundreds of points in a single session. The eyes of the world were on Wall Street, and Galleon was hitting on all cylinders. The firm paid millions of commission dollars to the Street, and in return, they were given fat allocations on new issues.

ZING! 25,000 shares of an IPO traded $60 higher.

SHAZZAM! 30,000 shares opened $40 higher than where it was priced.

POW! An oh-by-the way "kiss" from a second-tier broker looking to get in Galleon's good graces netted a nice six-figure sum.

It was my year, I thought. It had to be my year. As we edged toward the end of 1999, my relationship with the partners had never been better. The firm was killing it, and while the performance of my personal portfolio lagged, I had improved on the previous year. The value created by the options bets and hedges in the flagship fund spoke for itself, and my inclusion in their circle of trust was a mere formality.

Gary sat me down and my eyes began to spin like a slot machine. What would it be, a million? Two million? Three million?

"Todd," he began, "The partners appreciated your efforts this year. You did a good job. We're going to give you $50,000 as a token of our appreciation."

I knew what I had to do and understood what was at stake.

In the context of a multibillion dollar fund and hundreds of millions of dollars in cash on hand, 50 grand felt like a slap to the face. I immediately realized that if I was going to make real money on Wall Street, I had to step out from behind the shadows. If I was going to be a serious player, I had to be a partner. I asked Gary if that was in the cards, and he told me flat out that I didn't have what it took.

I beat myself up pretty badly after that meeting, questioning why I wasn't good enough, asking myself why I couldn't take that final step to stardom. It would be years later before I realized that not making partner at Galleon was the single best "failure" of my professional career.

When I left Morgan Stanley, David told me to make it count because you could only leave a firm that reputable once. The same could be said of Galleon; they were one of the top hedge funds in the world and nobody left on their own volition, but I knew what I had to do and understood what was at stake.

Once I left, that door would never be open again.

8

New Beginnings

It was the turn of the century and change was afoot. The stock market had soared to incredible heights, and there was plenty of gold on the horizon—I simply had to find my pot.

I had several conversations with Jim Cramer and Jeff Berkowitz during the final few months of 1999, and we were seemingly on the same page about me moving over to their shop. At $400 million, it was a much smaller fund than Galleon, but they dangled the elusive word: *partner*.

We met on several occasions to discuss the particulars of my term structure. I would join the firm and run the entire trading operation. My base salary would be $300,000, which provided the security I was looking for, but more enticing was that I would receive a nice percentage of the profits.

There was plenty of gold on the horizon—I simply had to find my pot.

Jim was wildly emotional, but from what I could tell, honest and fair. Jeff and I had become good friends through the years, and I came to know him as pragmatic and balanced. Jim and Jeff complemented each other as partners, and my skill-set figured to mesh equally well.

When I told Slaino of my plan, he asked me a simple question: "Do you trust them?" It was a simple yet critical criterion. Would they watch my back? Would they put my interests on par with their own? Would they do the right thing? I believed they would, and we met at the Gramercy Tavern in Manhattan to discuss the remaining details.

Cramer Berkowitz had a proven track record, beating their benchmark over the lifecycle of the fund, but recent years had proven more challenging, and they were looking to jumpstart their performance. I was coming from a different direction, but we all wanted the same thing, and it was hard to contain my enthusiasm as we discussed our future together.

The energy was palpable as we talked about the markets and the world at large. Jim continued to reference a financial website called TheStreet.com, which he co-founded in 1996 and took public in May 1999. I'd heard of it, but wasn't familiar with what it was or how it fit with the world of money management. I would soon find out, for better and for worse.

Lucky Charms

For those managing money at the beginning of 2000, the price action was nothing short of surreal. Each day was a journey, a volatile eruption of emotion that somehow morphed fantasy into reality at the end of each session. I couldn't have scripted a better beginning to my new endeavor of running the trading operation at Cramer Berkowitz. After a flurry of emotional buying following the Y2K scare, the NASDAQ dropped 450 points—11%—in a matter of days, and our desk gelled as if we had worked together for years.

Each day was a journey, a volatile eruption of emotion that somehow morphed fantasy into reality at the end of each session.

They say everything is funny when you're making money, and there were giggles all around as the ink dried on my contract. We were all on our best behavior, but make no mistake, we were a collection of distinctly powerful personalities with proven formulas for success. Jeff had a brilliant analytical mind, research director Matt Jacobs was plugged into the Street, Jim was a master of momentum, and I used volatility to my advantage, selling rallies and buying dips. When we were on the same page, it was akin to four chefs mixing the perfect brew. As we captured the violent market swings and dropped money into the till, we drank the sweet taste of success like nothing I had ever experienced.

In February 2000, Cramer penned his infamous "Winners of the New World" column on TheStreet.com, extolling the virtues of ten high-flying technology stocks. Each of them was sitting on a parabolic perch after a massive rally, but he believed they would continue higher and tried to convince us in kind. I tried to separate his online persona from our internal dynamic, sometimes successfully and other times not. Yet, our first few months were blissful as profits padded our portfolio, and while I struggled when I started at Morgan Stanley and Galleon, I was immediately at ease when I arrived each morning at the head of the desk.

I was ready to put my fingerprints on the operation and finally— *finally*—achieve the wealth and status that I had strived for my entire life.

As part of my charge, I was responsible for the implementation of risk management systems, commission allocation to our trading partners, and staffing decisions on the desk. The status quo that preceded my arrival would quickly change. I was ready to put my fingerprints on the operation and finally—*finally*—achieve the wealth and status that I had strived for my entire life.

The New Kid in Town

Our offices were on 40 Fulton Street, next to the Brooklyn Bridge and down the street from the World Trade Center and the New York Stock Exchange. It was the center of the financial universe and at the heart of the world's biggest cash register.

We had a dozen or so full-time employees, including three clerks who were directly under my charge. They had made multiple-six figure annual salaries for executing orders on behalf of Jim and Jeff, which seemed awfully extravagant given my experience. If I had learned anything climbing the ranks of Wall Street, it was that producers got paid and the pretenders faded away. It was the purest form of Darwinism; the strong survived, and the rest were left for dead.

I ushered in several changes during my first few months. The existing clerks were replaced with young guns that had skill-sets designed for the trading process, and while they weren't producers out of the gate, they had the talent to one day become stars, and eventually, most of them did. Further, while we actively traded $400 million, the profit or loss was calculated at the end of each session, and the actual performance—along with our trade errors—arrived from Goldman Sachs the *following* afternoon. That too, would have to evolve.

After ten years of paying dues, making salads, and being emasculated by my superiors, I was hungry and motivated.

After ten years of paying dues, making salads, and being emasculated by my superiors, I was hungry and motivated. I had promised myself that nobody who ever worked for me would be held down by internal office politics. I believed that the way to facilitate growth was to build a team with people who could themselves grow, and those decisions were made in kind.

I met with the desk heads of our various brokers—many of whom were the same folks who covered me at Galleon—and told them that commission revenue would be correlated to their idea generation and the liquidity they provided. It was indeed a meritocracy; we were tough but fair and always operated within the letter of the law. We were everything that a hedge fund was supposed to be and more. It was, I thought at the time, professional nirvana.

All a man has is his name and his word. The trading operation at Cramer Berkowitz evolved into a direct extension of that.

Word of our approach quickly spread and our firm hummed like a well-oiled machine. We got one of the first calls from our brokers when their analysts changed the rating on a stock; head traders communicated the directional flow from their "smarter" accounts, and I always shared what we were seeing in an attempt to establish goodwill.

We treated people the way I had wanted to be treated when I was on the other end of the phone. We always told them why we traded and rarely, if ever, hurt them with our flow. If we ran over them with one of our orders—if they didn't have an opportunity to hedge our risk—we adjusted the price of the transaction as a matter of course.

All a man has is his name and his word. The trading operation at Cramer Berkowitz evolved into a direct extension of that.

Wild Pitches

Feeling emboldened in the spring of 2000, I swung at a pitch that was outside my strike zone. One of our brokers had alerted me to a special situation, a stock called Focus Enhancements that he believed was ready to run. We were making money, and as I was trading particularly well Jim and Jeff were happy to indulge me.

After we collectively weighed the opportunity, we established a six-figure position as the stock traded between $6 and $8. We were in

a groove and our confidence was matched only by our growing reputation. With the market swinging wildly—10% to 15% at a clip—we
seemingly had the script in our hands before the market moved, and
by the middle of the first quarter, we established a sizable lead on the
averages. We were feeling particularly bold.

Then the twitching started, a facial tick that would become all too familiar with time.

"Focus Enhancements on the tape!" screamed Matt Jacobs as we
trained our eyes on the headline. The news was negative, and the
stock dropped 30% before we took our next breath.

Nobody said a word as the phones rang unanswered, and Maria
Bartiromo chattered away in the background. I was frozen—we all
were—despite the fact that the loss, while substantial, was a pimple in
the much broader complexion of our $400 million portfolio. I sat
across from Jim and watched his face turn from white to pink to a
sullen shade of red, and then the twitching started, a facial tick that
would become all too familiar with time. He pushed back from his
turret and walked into his office. Instinctively, Jeff, Matt, and I followed and shut the door behind us.

I've always been my own harshest critic, and I held myself to the
highest standards. Nobody needed to tell me I had screwed up. They
knew it, I knew it, we all knew it. But this was one trade—a big trade,
but one trade—in the context of a series of profitable decisions that
netted our firm millions of dollars. I braced for some backlash but
wasn't prepared for what followed. Jim was relatively calm at first, but
what began as a discussion regarding our alternatives to either miti-
gate risk or seize an opportunity quickly devolved into a soapbox rant.

Just as bad seasons define good fans and bad times define good friends, bad trades define the true colors of your partners in the pits.

It stopped being a dialogue between partners—Jim unleashed in a way that I had never before seen. All he could do was detail how horrible and unacceptable the situation was, over and over and over again, incessantly harping on the mistake rather than trying to identify a solution. He screamed. He swore. I may have even seen a tear by the time he was done. It was the strangest display of emotion I had ever witnessed in a professional setting or elsewhere.

By the time I left his office, I wasn't thinking about Focus Enhancements. All I could think was, "Who is this guy and what the hell just happened?"

I've worked with some serious personalities over the years: Chuck Feldman was a powerful force, and Gary Rosenbach was difficult in an entirely different way, but what I witnessed that day set a new standard and provided a valuable lesson. Just as bad seasons define good fans and bad times define good friends, bad trades define the true colors of your partners in the pits.

9

Battle Lines

My grandfather once told me to keep my right hand up. As a former Golden Gloves boxer, that was his way of telling me to protect my chin. After Jim's emotional tirade, I never walked through that office the same way again. I knew that I was only as good as my last trade, but at Cramer Berkowitz, that expression was taken to an entirely new level. It wasn't enough to be right; you had to be right all the time, every day.

It was March 2000 and the NASDAQ had rallied 35% in a little over a month. Jeff and Matt scoured corporate America as Jim and I, sitting five feet apart and facing each other, moved mountains and molehills from dusk till dawn.

My grandfather once told me to keep my right hand up.

While we shared a common mission, our styles were drastically different. Jim, as a momentum trader, warmed to stocks once they rallied and cooled after they fell. As a function of my facilitation roots at Morgan Stanley, I preferred to "fade" the market, buying dips and selling blips. Our stylistic dichotomy was a high stakes game of chicken and somebody was bound to blink.

I remember precisely when the moment of clarity arrived. Tech stocks were rallying 10, 30, 50 points in a single day, and I awoke in the middle of the night with a disturbing epiphany. It wasn't the first time I had the thought, but it was different that time, a clarity that seemed obvious, a crystallization that would define my career. The technology bubble was about to burst.

One of the toughest disciplines to master when trading is to unwind a position that is making money. Multiply that dynamic by a large portfolio, add a slew of zeros, and factor in the emotional dysfunction of our office, and you'll get a sense of the task at hand.

I won't say I was the lone bear—Jeff also sensed wreckage on the horizon—but the timing, coupled with the intensely competitive landscape, made for prickly friction with a razor thin margin of error. Jim summed it up in his first book, *Confessions of a Street Addict*, when he wrote: "When April came in, and the NASDAQ was still in the 4,500 area, Todd suggested that we were on the verge of a collapse of titanic proportions, that the whole NASDAQ bubble was about to burst and would shortly be at 1,500."

The tension was thick, and as the new kid on the block, I knew where the loyalties lay.

Now, you've got to understand Jim. He had a genuinely kind heart and always strived to do the right thing, but he could make your life miserable if you were on the wrong side of his mind. Jeff used to muse that if Jim hit someone with a car and you politely informed him of the accident, he would drive the victim to the hospital and buy the entire family dinner. If you told Jim he screwed up, he would raise his arms and scream, "Shut up or I'll hit you, too!"

Such was life at Cramer Berkowitz in the weeks before what was at the time the largest car crash in financial history. It wasn't enough that I had a strong sense the wheels were about to fall off the financial wagon, I had to explain why the timing was right and do it with tact. Gut feels and hairs on the back of my neck weren't enough, and heaven help me if we missed further upside or worse, got squeezed on the short side. The tension was thick, and as the new kid on the block, I knew where the loyalties lay.

Pop Goes the Weasel

April 2000 arrived with a bang, and the NASDAQ dropped 20% in a few short sessions. What's more, as we actively traded the volatility, we caught the countertrend rally back to NASDAQ 4500 before again riding the short side to fresh market lows. The markets crashed all around us, and we were in the eye of the storm, an island of clarity in an otherwise unsure world.

We posted huge gains, paid the Street insane commissions, and the trading staff and risk-management protocol I implemented had paid huge dividends. The swings were wild, $20 million, $30 million in a single session, the type of numbers that you didn't want to comprehend. Our new systems updated our P&L dynamically, and we knew exactly where we stood with each flickering tick. That was both a blessing and a curse. I didn't need to watch my screens, as the look on Jim's face across the desk told the story in real-time.

Any trader who says that he or she doesn't take performance personally shouldn't be managing money. We ran one portfolio—hundreds of positions that forged a single bottom line—but we each had our "names." While we all played for the same team, we each eyeballed our individual stats as we went home each night.

It was the best of times; it was the worst of times. It was functional, dysfunctional, friendly, heated, seamless, and strangely sophomoric all at the same time.

The inherent differences between our individual trading approaches became increasingly apparent. When the market rallied, Jim tossed fresh long exposure into our portfolio. After it reversed lower, sometimes minutes later, short positions would suddenly appear on our sheets. I watched him closely and traded my positions with an eye toward the overall risk profile. I wasn't worried about stepping on toes or honoring the status quo. After coming so close in my two previous professional endeavors, I had two missions in life: to make money and to protect those gains.

As the summer approached, we operated at a feverish pitch and harnessed that energy into tremendous performance. Still, there was an unspoken angst in the office, the type of tension that was only acceptable if we beat the Street.

It was the best of times; it was the worst of times. It was functional, dysfunctional, friendly, heated, seamless, and strangely sophomoric all at the same time. It was life at Cramer Berkowitz, and unbeknownst to me, we were about to open our window to the world.

A Worldwide Window

The fuel injected ascent of technology stocks—the unintended consequences of Alan Greenspan's policy following the Asian contagion—was unwinding at a rapid pace, and we were making a lot of money. To the outside looking in, our fund was the definition of lucidity, but internally, a different dynamic began to take shape.

As Jim readied for a summer vacation in the Hamptons, he was on the phone with his editor at TheStreet.com looking for someone to write his column while he was away. When his eyes locked on mine, I saw a light bulb flash above his head as a grin spread across his face. "I've got it covered. Toddo will write on Monday while you find someone for the rest of the week."

I was trading 200 positions and managing $400 million worth of risk, and I didn't want another job—my hands were full as it was. I said to Jim, "Dude, it's not happening. The last time I wrote something was to my mother while at summer camp." But he had already made up his mind; his problem was solved, and it quickly became mine.

I didn't put much thought into my first column. I scribed Grateful Dead lyrics that pertained to the tape, threaded in some levity through pop culture references, and espoused my bearish bent in real-time, delving into the details of my particular trading approach. I didn't initially embrace the double duty, but surprisingly, it didn't bother me either. In fact, I found that it helped crystallize my thoughts as I tried to navigate the wicked crosscurrents of the marketplace in real-time.

As the closing bell approached on Monday, July 3, 2000, I got a call from the editor at TheStreet.com asking me to finish the week. "Sure," I said as I looked at Jeff and smiled. "Anything I can do to help."

The Switch Is Flipped

There was no middle ground with Jim. Every day was either the best ever or the worst imaginable. That applied to his personal relationships as well: You were either his close friend or a sworn enemy. I toggled between the two, often in the same day, but there was little doubt about which side of his emotional chasm I was on when I pulled up to his East End rental on Friday night. "Toddo!" he screamed as he ran down the driveway and wrapped me in a bear hug. "We gotta talk!"

I was with a friend who was stunned by the outburst of emotion, and I couldn't blame her; Hurricane Jim was frenzied energy that swallowed everything in his path. She didn't know the other side of his mental ride, but it was just as well; she wouldn't have believed it anyway. He excitedly told me that my columns performed fantastically well. That surprised me, but I had little time to digest the news—he had a plan, and his wheels were already spinning. "We're going to give you a trading diary on TheStreet.com right next to mine. It'll be great! Whadaya say?"

Uncle Buck, Young Frankenstein, Led Zeppelin, and Jimi Hendrix commingled with my stock market analysis into a single stream of consciousness.

What could I say? I had never shied from a challenge, and I'm not sure that I could have if I had wanted to. To be honest, I'm not sure that I wanted to. I actually enjoyed writing, if only for the opportunity to synthesize my thoughts and move my mind in a different direction. I had no way of knowing that Jim opened a door for me that would forever change my life.

I promised myself that I wouldn't let the column splinter the focus that was quietly lining my pockets. Writing came naturally, however, and soon became a seamless part of a cohesive duopoly that opened a world to me that I never knew existed. Uncle Buck, Young Frankenstein, Led Zeppelin, and Jimi Hendrix commingled with my stock market analysis into a single stream of consciousness.

At first, I feared the additional responsibility would add tension to an already strained environment. While Jim and I often disagreed on how to approach the market, that friction was behind closed doors. Now, through the power of the Internet, our approach was at odds for the world to see.

Interestingly, that's not what happened. TheStreet.com was Jim's baby, perhaps in a more profound way than the hedge fund. As my page views increased and our performance percolated, I noticed a cumulative kinship. I didn't realize his motivation at the time, but it made perfect sense. TheStreet.com was a very personal project for Jim; it was his name, and they were his words.

The stock market volatility continued to weed out the weak hands and punish those who confused brains with a bubble. One of the first lessons I learned when trading was that you must adapt your style to the market, and the wild ride of the Internet bubble was a lesson in discipline and agility. By the time the crowd got to the "right" side of the trade, the market shifted in the other direction, leaving blood in its wake. There was carnage all around us, from famous hedge fund managers shuttering their doors to mainstream Americans suddenly caught under a waterfall of supply.

We all wanted the same thing— performance....

My guttural instinct was to insulate our fund from the crimson tide that swallowed the Street, and I began to view Jim's momentum-style approach as a contrary indicator, subconsciously at first and then with increased frequency. As our fund outperformed and I embraced the column he enabled me to attain, I swallowed my tongue and kept the peace. He was still the boss; he was still Jim Cramer.

I didn't dislike him, and in fact, I had tremendous respect for his intelligence and cared greatly for him as a friend. Beneath his wild emotional swings beat a genuinely tender heart. We all wanted the same thing—performance—and I pushed through our problems despite the increasingly frequent clashes over how we approached our risk profile.

As we edged through the back half of 2000, it was clear something was going to give, and that something wasn't going to be me.

10

Reality Bites

It would be easy to dislike Jim if he didn't have that childlike giddiness to him. Anyone who knows him understands what I'm talking about. Beneath the surface of his public persona, he's every bit a little kid who wants to be liked. His warmth and generosity were treasured occurrences, and when they appeared, animosity magically dissipated into a melting pot of goodwill. I didn't understand the mood swings at first but when I finally did, it would be with more empathy than acrimony.

I got a call in the middle of the trading day in 2000 when we were actively moving merchandise back and forth, steadily making profits and rewarding our investors. The mood on our desk was intense as the market slid down a slippery slope.

"Hello, can I speak to Todd Harrison please?" said an unfamiliar voice on the other end of the phone. After a brief exchange, the bomb dropped. The call was from the Maui Correctional Facility and was about my father. As I sat back in my chair and listened, I learned that my dad had been homeless, was abusing drugs, and was being held in jail in solitary confinement. It had been almost ten years since we last spoke. *Ten years.* A lot happened in my life during that time, and evidently a lot happened to him as well.

As the head trader of a large trading operation, I was able to make quick and emotionless decisions on the fly. However, on that day in 2000, I was suddenly numb to the flickering ticks that surrounded me.

I'll never forget that moment. We were in a dogfight in the middle of a financial crisis, and the most competitive person I've ever met urged me to go to Hawaii to take care of my father.

Jim, immediately sensing something was wrong, motioned me to his office behind him. I walked into the glass-enclosed room and sat on the couch across from his desk. Jeff filed in behind me and asked what happened. I explained the situation, or at least what I knew of it, and Jim didn't skip a beat. "Go to Maui," he said. "Take care of what you need to take care of."

I'll never forget that moment. We were in a dogfight in the middle of a financial crisis, and the most competitive person I've ever met urged me to go to Hawaii to take care of my father.

By the time I digested what he suggested, he was already on the phone making calls on my behalf. He contacted an investor in our fund who had connections in Hawaii, and within a few short hours, I had retained one of the best lawyers in Maui, had flights scheduled, and had a hotel booked. All that was left was to face my father, who was 5,000 miles away from the safety and security of the life I had built.

The Other Side of the Rainbow

Not wanting to take the trip alone, I asked my brother to join me. Two days later, Adam and I landed in Maui and drove to the lawyer's office. We had both given up on our dad, but felt compelled to do something; he was our father, and we were his last line of defense.

The attorney filled us in on the situation. Our dad, homeless for years, had panhandled on the street and worn out his welcome wherever he went. He was arrested for impersonating a police officer and, once in jail, had attacked one of the guards, who then beat him and placed him in solitary confinement. We were told our father had smeared blood all over his cell in an act of defiance. It was, and remains, surreal.

The following morning, we sat in the Maui Courthouse and awaited arraignment. As the judge called the session to order, the bailiff led a string of defendants into the room. I couldn't find my father. The orange jumpsuits looked the same, and the chains that bound them together distracted me. I scanned the group twice and focused on a gaunt man in the middle of the pack with gangly facial hair and tattoos. *Dad?*

His emotionless eyes rose to mine, and I saw the man I once knew—the man who abandoned our family, the man who proudly drove a Ferrari as a sign of arrival, the man who moved to Hawaii to find his slice of paradise. He was broken and had hit rock bottom.

Over the course of the following week, Adam and I visited scattered locations throughout Maui and picked up the pieces of our dad's displaced life. The other side of paradise, we discovered, was a harsh place indeed. He had left a trail of debt, desperation, and dereliction that seemingly had no end. Our father had joined a cult and signed away his possessions. Once banished from there, he had wandered the island in search of handouts. He had slipped into resorts and pretended to be part of a seminar so he could get hot coffee and a roll. He had his golden retriever Bubba fetch rocks from the ocean in return for loose change from tourists.

We drove from one situation to the next, like mice in a maze, unsure of what we would find at the next stop. Our father had thousands of dollars of debt and owed people favors, many of whom looked at us to settle up. We also discovered he was a sick man who suffered through many years of an undetected and untreated bipolar disorder.

That stuck in my mind. *He was a sick man.*

During our final day in Maui, Adam and I visited our dad in jail. He apologized for everything he did and didn't do. I recalled birthdays that I spent glancing toward the phone waiting for calls that never came. It had been an emotional week, one that opened wounds I believed were long closed.

As we sat in his cell, he broke down and told us he had nothing to live for, and that he had contemplated suicide many times. My brother took from his pocket a picture of his two children, my niece and nephew, and handed it to our father. "This is what you have to look forward to," he said, his gesture catching me off guard.

"Yes, Dad," I continued. "If you stay clean, we'll help you get back on track, pay off your debts, find a home…. you'll get to meet your grandchildren."

I could see the guards watching from the corner of my eye, and I wanted them to soak it in. Perhaps they would think twice about beating him if they knew that he was a father and a grandfather. I gave him my word I would return in one year to resume our relationship, that we would sit outside and watch the Maui sunset, as a strange emotion washed over my body, one of relief.

He was a sick man, I again thought to myself. *It wasn't my fault.*

Fitting the Pieces Together

On the one side of my life, there was a volatile man, Jim Cramer, who swung between the depths of despair and heights of giddy happiness. On the other, there was my father, who suffered from bipolar disorder and exacerbated his illness by self-medicating.

As I discussed my father's diagnosis with Jim, I arrived at a startling revelation. Cramer, as brilliant as he was, with his photographic memory, with his uncanny ability to retain information, suffered from a similar disorder as my father. Jim spoke openly about the ailment, and assured me the condition could be treated with proper medication. His counsel was extremely helpful and much appreciated.

Jim Cramer and my father led very different lives, but a common denominator bound them and, by extension, me. Perhaps Jim's condition should have been more apparent, but it's not something one looks for. Following my awareness of my dad's affliction and Jim's benevolence in helping me navigate it, I developed newfound respect for the man. We connected in a way that is tough to describe—I got him, and I suppose he got me.

Every day was a game of mental chess, and we knew how to push each other's buttons, rarely if ever missing an opportunity to do so.

I also realized that, much like my father, his emotional swings weren't preceded with conscious intent. As his friend, I found myself rooting for his happiness and wellbeing. As his partner tasked with managing $400 million of risk, we continued to battle over every dollar in our ever-changing P&L, with Jeff often serving as the balanced mediator.

The constant vacillation took a toll, tangibly and intangibly, as we edged through the remainder of 2000. Every day was a game of mental chess, and we knew how to push each other's buttons, rarely if ever missing an opportunity to do so. Admittedly, my empathy sometimes took a backseat to the frustration that surrounded his seemingly haphazard decision-making process.

There were two movies playing at the same time. The online relationship, where a loyal following watched our drastically different stylistic approaches, drew huge traffic for TheStreet.com. Inside the office, as we raced toward our payday, the dynamic was far from stable. Our lead over the mainstay averages grew, and we were up 20-something percent, 40% higher than our benchmark, but success was bittersweet, and nothing seemed to satiate the intense desire to lengthen our lead.

I reminded myself of a subtle yet important fact. Our gains were on paper, they didn't matter until we locked them in, and I wasn't getting paid until Jim signed the check. After my experiences at Morgan Stanley and Galleon, I wasn't about to take anything for granted.

11

Sign of the Times

In late 2000, Jim asked if I would join him at TheStreet.com conference, followed by dinner with Gene Hackman. I jumped at the opportunity to meet and dine with one of my favorite actors, and told Jim I would go if I didn't have to speak at the conference. Writing was one thing, but speaking in front of thousands of people wasn't something I was interested in. He gave me his word that I would remain in the periphery, and I happily tagged along.

The grand ballroom at the Marriott World Trade Center was standing room only—I had never seen anything like it. Investors swarmed Jim during the cocktail hour asking for stock picks and market advice. I stuffed my nametag in my pocket and tried to remain invisible.

Jim gave the keynote speech as the audience furiously scribbled on their notepads. I watched him work the room and thought to myself, he's good—he's, a masterful marketer. During the Q&A that followed his speech, someone asked about options pricing. "You know," he began, "I can answer that, but I have someone in the room who trades options better than anyone I know. You all know my head trader, Toddo 'Cookie' Harrison, right? Why don't we have Todd come up here? Whadaya say, Toddo?"

When a two-time Academy Award winner is standing alone in a crowded ballroom, and a trader is mobbed like a film star, there's something very wrong with the mainstream mindset.

My teeth clenched as a few people began to clap, and before long, the entire audience was cheering for me to step up to the podium. I had no choice—I was no longer invisible. I slowly walked on stage, answered the question, fielded several more, and then returned to my seat.

Some people have a fear of public speaking, but I won't lie, in a way, I enjoyed it. Perhaps it offered validation that I subconsciously sought after being abandoned as a child. Maybe I, too, had a desire to be liked. I don't fully understand the reasoning; I can only communicate the feeling I experienced at the time.

When the conference concluded, I desperately had to use the men's room, but realized it would be difficult to make my way through the crowd. Within minutes, I was surrounded—there were eight, ten people circling me like a bulls-eye on an archery target.

"What do you think of Cisco?"

"What's your favorite financial short?"

"Where will the S&P end this year?"

I was overwhelmed. I didn't have time to digest one question before being pelted with another, and I still had to pee. I looked over the crowd and saw Gene Hackman checking his watch. When a two-time Academy Award winner is standing alone in a crowded ball-room, and a trader is mobbed like a film star, there's something very wrong with the mainstream mindset.

This stock market movie was not going to end well.

The Moment of Truth

Jeff was at the First Boston conference in late November feeding us tremendous insight about the technology companies that were presenting. After ten years of friendship and close-knit interaction in the office, he and I had arrived at a place of instinctive intuitiveness, and I executed upon his thoughts before words were ever exchanged. We had a rhythm that bridged his analytical reasoning with my trad-ing gut; we were everything that hedge fund partners were supposed to be, and more.

As Jeff shared his bearish inclinations on Microsoft from the hall-way of the conference, I was on the horn with Deutsche Bank, which had a large institutional buyer of the stock. I was looking for an excuse to take a short position, and Jeff delivered it in spades.

Bang! We're short two-fifty (250,000 shares) and covered it down a buck.

Zing! Puts were flowing like water in and out of our green portfolio.

Pow! Another facial tick by Microsoft CFO John Connors, and we tossed a few hundred thousand shares back out.

We had yet to eat lunch, and Mr. Softee alone had netted us close to three million dollars, and it wasn't just Microsoft that made money as we hosted a profit party at Cramer Berkowitz. We opened our stance and took a full cut, and we coined money across the board in tech. We traded so much merchandise with so many brokers that our team barely had time to input the positions into our risk management system. It was the definition of fluidity as our daily P&L grew from three to four to five million.

As the market close approached, I felt a great sense of satisfaction. We played to win and exhibited the discipline that is the hallmark of any great trading operation. It would have been a perfect session if not for the tiny landmine nestled between the sheets. You see, in the midst of those multiple seven-figure wins was a 20,000-share position in the computer storage company Brocade. It was one of the best performing stocks at the time and as an extension one of Jim's favorites as well. I hadn't even seen him enter into the position.

I had seen that movie before and wasn't interested in watching the sequel.

After the closing bell, Brocade announced a picture perfect quarter, a work of art in an otherwise burning building—they nailed it. Unfortunately, the stock was trading well over $100 per share, and the good news was already baked into the price.

Blink, and it was down five. Sigh, and it was down $10.

With each draft lower, Jim nibbled on more stock, and with each downtick, Mount Vesuvius growled louder on the other side of the desk.

I tried to calm Jim by pointing to our monster session. "Relax brother," I said. "We had a huge day." But he didn't want to hear it. The venom was thick as spit flew from his mouth, and he smashed his phone and keyboard against the desk, over and over and over again.

I had seen that movie before and wasn't interested in watching the sequel. I got up, grabbed my jacket from the back of my chair and walked out. I heard an object, which I would later learn was a water bottle, smash against the closed door while I waited for the elevator. As far as I was concerned, I wasn't going to return as long as Mr. Cramer was there.

Jim called Jeff to complain that I didn't care about the fund. A bit later, Jeff called me, and we had a long conversation.

Victory Laps and Big Steps Back

Life at Cramer Berkowitz was like living in a reality show. I only wish someone had the foresight to film it. Jim's focus increasingly shifted toward his growing media presence on TheStreet.com and CNBC, which was fine by me—the clock was ticking toward a rather large payday, and the end of the year couldn't arrive fast enough. His ability to juggle so many tasks was an amazing accomplishment, but at the time I viewed his attention as splintered at best.

One day, I yelled across the desk to Jim as he leaned back in his chair with the phone pressed against his ear and alerted him that we were making a big bet against the market. When he saw me vying for his attention, he gave me a thumbs-up, placed his hand over the receiver and said, "I love 'em here—go!" After I informed him we were aggressively shorting the tape—betting in the opposite direction—he nodded his head in agreement and made "selling gestures" with his hands as if to say "Sell, sell, sell!"

I have no agenda in sharing the details of this interaction. As we edged toward the end of 2000, however, I had tremendous motivation to finish the year and get our investors—and myself—paid. Jim was a living, breathing rollercoaster, and I desperately wanted to get off.

As year-end flickered in the distance, we collectively made a decision to trade less, sit on our outsized gains and ride out the calendar. It was a prudent decision given our substantial lead and the uncertainty surrounding the market, and we pared our book to minimal risk and agreed to trade only the very best edges.

When Push Comes to Shove

Our process at the fund was constant; we walked through our portfolio multiple times each day and manicured our risk profile as a function of time and price. We did this through good times and bad, and it was a discipline that sustained us regardless of market conditions. It was the best way to keep a collection of ADD portfolio managers on the same page during our sensory-overloaded journey.

A funny thing happened with our newfound risk management approach—positions began to mysteriously appear as we chewed through our skeletal sheets. While Jim insisted his sources were "giving him the wink," Jeff and I would muse and imagine, via Instant Message, who some of his "sources" might be.

Genghis Kahn, perhaps?

How about Abe Lincoln?

Ty Cobb?

It was a little funny and a bit sad, but it didn't matter. On a $400,000,000 tank, those positions were rubber bullets that quietly bounced off the armor of our relative performance.

Something was definitely afoot as we swallowed the dings of edgeless risk and waffled our way toward our year-end payday.

As I looked ahead, I wasn't as ambivalent. We had the makings of a legitimate all-star squad, and while I had only worked with Jim for one year, I no longer had an interest in sitting on the other side of his mood swings. It was a delicate balance; I genuinely cared for him as a friend—he was there for me when I needed him—but the professional dynamic had become untenable.

Additionally, my grandfather's health began to deteriorate, a sad reality that I needed to tend to. Perhaps I was selfish or maybe a bit greedy when I began to calculate what the payout pie would look like if Jim were removed from the equation, and once that thought began to germinate, it was difficult to shake. I spoke with Jeff and Matt and shared my desire to leave at the end of the year. Our instant messages flickered more quickly, and the outside phone calls increased in frequency. Yes, something was definitely afoot as we swallowed the dings of edgeless risk and waffled our way toward our year-end payday.

As the emotional fervor came to a head, Cramer Berkowitz arrived at the fateful day that would forever change our lives.

Behind the Closed Door

I don't know what was discussed during the hour Jim Cramer and Jeff Berkowitz huddled in Jim's office toward the end of 2000, but time stood still as I watched them from the other side of the glass wall.

I had a serious heart-to-heart with Jeff the night of the Brocade tirade when Jim destroyed keyboards and threw a water bottle at me as I walked out of the office. I had told Jeff that night that as much as I appreciated the opportunity and was grateful to Jim for the friendship in my time of need, I didn't want to return the following year if he was there. Jeff wasn't surprised—my frustration had been obvious since the end of the third quarter—but that was the first time I put it out there. "I'll talk to him," he said at the time. "Just relax and show up tomorrow."

Jeff is a good man who lives his life by example, and he had more on the line than the rest of us combined, nine hard years of channeling information to Jim and quietly feeding his stardom. Loyalty is a rare quality on Wall Street; Jeff lived it and I knew it. I suppose that, more than anything else was in the back of my mind as I waited for them to emerge from Jim's office.

The door flew open and Jim bounded into the trading room at a quickened pace. At first, I couldn't tell if he was angry or ecstatic, which was apropos given the fine line that separated the two emotions in the man. He stepped up to the front of the trading desk and a hush fell over the firm. This was it, I thought to myself at the time, the moment of truth.

"I've made a decision," he said as the corners of his lips folded upward into a smile. "At the end of this year, I'm going to announce my retirement and hand the firm over to Jeff."

My eyes connected with Berko as I began to digest the news. And then it hit me—Jeff was the one who told me the car crash analogy; he's the one who taught me that you don't talk *at* Jim, you talk *with* him.

I assumed that Jeff communicated his desire to step out from behind Cramer's shadow and take his shot as the man in charge. I'm unsure of how large a role I played in Jeff's decision to have that discussion—or Jim's reaction, knowing that my loyalties were with Jeff—but it didn't really matter. Much like trading, all that counted was the bottom line.

Perception and Reality

The mood was generally positive as we spoke of Jim's legacy. He would often joke, "Gretzky, Elway, Jordan—Cramer!" And we ran with it. The man had a heck of a run as a hedge fund manager, and it was fitting that he wrote his own swan song.

Jim knew that he could leverage his track record into a successful media career, and he had already made inroads with CNBC. His stated stance was that he wanted to spend more time with his family and that he had tired of the sleepless nights and vicious competition that were the necessary evils of money management. It seemed like the best-case scenario. He was happy, and we were happy; it was perfect.

My initial relief morphed into a more pressing question. If Jim left the business, what would he claim as his final payday when we whacked up the bonus pool? I was guaranteed a set portion of the profits, but given my relative contribution to the performance, I believed I was entitled to a larger percentage. After a string of year-end disappointments, I had finally hit the lottery. It couldn't be happening again. Could it?

We stopped trading for the final month of the year, sitting on a 28% gain while the rest of the Street swallowed sizable losses, and spent most of our time chewing through the logistics of transferring full ownership of the firm to Jeff. I was excited for Berko as he earned the right to helm his own operation, and I was excited for myself as I prepared to assume the role of president, a title previously held by Jim.

I was finally on the other side of the cash register.

That, and a $700,000 annual salary with a two-year guarantee, had harnessed me into a positive place. I sat down with Jeff to discuss the final compensation allocation for 2000, and he assured me that I would be taken care of in a manner consistent with my performance. True to his word, I was.

While Jim secured a sizable chunk of change as his final payday on Wall Street, I netted close to $5 million, which was considerably more than I was contractually due. A new era began at Cramer Berkowitz, and I finally shook the monkey off my back.

I was finally on the other side of the cash register.

.

12

Brokedown Palace

It was a beautiful, crisp September morning as I looked up from my *Wall Street Journal* to watch the sunrise over the East River. It was a peaceful moment, and I paused to reflect on the beauty of the landscape and my place in life. That was the first thing I remember about 9/11, how sharp the horizon was as day broke over lower Manhattan.

Our hedge fund was bearish on the macro landscape but positioned for a countertrend upside trade heading into that session. As I settled into my turret and downed a second cup of coffee, Nokia preannounced a negative quarter—they released news that business was worse than expected—and the stock shot 5% higher. It was a telltale sign that the market was washed out, proof positive that traders had bet on further declines and were being forced to buy back their negative exposure. We pressed the upside, furiously buying the S&P and NASDAQ, and twisted the knife into the sides of the bears who had overstayed their welcome.

The first boom shook our office walls. I scanned the traders sitting around my trading desk and said, "What the hell was that?"

Jeff's brother yelled, "The World Trade Center's on fire!" We turned to the towers and saw flames and black smoke billowing into the clear blue sky.

At 40 Fulton Street, we were a few short blocks away, and, on the 24th floor, we had a bird's-eye view. The mainstream media had yet to pick up the story, which only added to the confusion as we watched it unfold in real-time. I instinctively turned to write on TheStreet.com, posting commentary at 8:47 a.m. "A bomb has exploded in the WTC. May God have mercy on those innocent souls."

The S&P and NASDAQ futures traded wildly in ten, twenty handle clips. We made some sales, but when it was reported that a small commuter plane had crashed, we scooped back that inventory back and then some. All of this occurred in a matter of minutes, if that.

I've since learned that the reason we couldn't look away from the towers was that our minds had no way to process the information. That, no matter how hard we tried to mentally digest what we saw, there was nowhere to "file" images of human beings holding hands and jumping from atop the World Trade Center. It's an image I can't shake to this day, bodies falling through a maze of confetti like ants from a tree. It's a sight that I wish to God I had never seen.

We huddled by our window with our mouths gaped open as somebody repeated "Oh my God!" over and over again. The second plane circled behind the tower and entered it from behind. In slow motion, the impact shook the foundation of our building as the fireball exploded directly toward us. I thought to myself "This is how I'm going to die," as we gathered our staff and ushered them toward the stairwell. I stopped by my turret, quickly wrote, "I'm evacuating our building...." and sent it to my editors, unsure if they would ever receive it.

The Duck and Cover

We left our building and ran toward the South Street Seaport. I remember thinking that, worst case, we could dive in the East River and take our chances there. We overheard someone say that the Pentagon was attacked. The Pentagon? Weren't missiles supposed to shoot down anything that threatened that air space? The Verizon switching center had been damaged, and we had no cell phones or Blackberries or any voice of reason to assuage our fears. We were cut off from the world.

I remember thinking that, worst case, we could dive in the East River and take our chances there.

I thought of friends who worked in the towers. I resisted the urge to run to Ground Zero to find them and tried to put on a brave face to calm my shaken staff.

The crumbling began with a whisper and grew to a growl as the first tower imploded. We naturally assumed another wave of attacks had begun. Everyone scrambled and scattered our office among thousands of other confused people as the wave of white smoke approached.

I'm not sure how Jeff and I found each other, but we somehow connected and ran along the river toward FDR Drive. I eyed the water to our right as a precaution—it was an option that I wanted to keep open as we broke into a sprint.

How could I ease her pain? What was happening to our country? Was it really happening at all?

We somehow flagged down a taxi, and Jeff offered the driver $500 to take him out of the city while I tried to calm the woman in the backseat who was on the verge of hyperventilation. Between gasps, she told me that her boyfriend worked in an office high up in the World Trade Center. As I looked out the back window and saw that one of the towers was already gone, I was at a loss for words. How could I ease her pain? What was happening to our country? Was it really happening at all?

I made my way to my home on 57th Street as lines formed at convenience stores in my neighborhood. People were hoarding bottled water, canned food, flashlights, and other necessities. I had none of that, and I didn't care; I just wanted to find my family and my friends. I needed to understand what had happened and establish a framework of relativity, a place where I could begin to digest and assess my experience. The images on TV portrayed downtown Manhattan as a cloud of smoke; a disaster area with body parts strewn like yesterday's laundry on the bedroom floor.

Thirty minutes later, my mother charged through my front door and held me tighter than I've ever been held. Soon thereafter, friends began to gather at my apartment; there were five at first, then ten, then twenty. It was a dose of humanity in a sea of horror, a refuge of comfort in a maze of confusion. I found myself sitting at my living room desk, looking for a semblance of normalcy and a familiar setting.

Instinctively, I wrote this column, which was published on TheStreet.com.

The Day the World Changed
By Todd Harrison
09/11/2001 08:33 PM EDT

Numbness. Shock. Anger. Sadness.

As I sit here with family and friends, awaiting calls that may never come, I am drawn to my keyboard and I'm not quite sure why.

Perhaps it's an attempt to somehow release the tremendous sadness that's locked inside me. Maybe I have hopes that sharing my grief will stop these images...stop the shaking.

It's ten hours after the fact, and I still feel the "boom" that shook my trading room.

I can still see the bodies falling from the first struck tower, one after another, as we gathered by the window in shock and confusion.

I can still hear the screams in my office "Oh my God! Oh my God! Oh my God!" as the second plane hit...and the image of that fireball rolling toward us will forever be etched in my mind.

I often write that "this too shall pass," but I will never be the same. Maybe that's a selfish thought, as tens of thousands of people won't have the opportunity to put this behind them.

Each time my phone rings and I hear the voice of a friend who I feared was lost, I break into tears.

Every time I get a call from someone who "just wanted to make sure" I'm still here, I'm reminded of how lucky I am to share relationships, memories and a past.

I know many of you read my column to make money, but do yourself a favor and surround yourself with loved ones this evening.

Some of the wealthiest people I know don't have two dimes to rub together, and a few of them will never see their children, parents or friends again.

More than anything else, I wish I'd kept my date to share a drink with my good friend at Cantor Fitz.

I was tired, opting to grab a good night's sleep rather than down a couple of apple martinis with my sage friend.

I'm sitting by my phone, brother, waiting for your call.

Drinks are on me.

Picking Up the Pieces

People who shared a similar 9/11 experience dealt with their grief differently. Some left the business entirely, opting to enjoy a life where bells didn't bookend their days. Some married, and others divorced as the specter of death shifted their path in life. Still others fell into drug and alcohol addictions, with hopes that self-medication would dull their pain. We each did what we could; we all did what we had to.

I was numb and relied on instincts to make it from hour to hour and day to day. CNN asked me to appear on television that weekend, and while I didn't want to be in the public eye I decided that my message needed to be heard: Stay calm, don't make emotional decisions, and remain patient. I believed that the downdraft that would inevitably occur when global markets reopened would ultimately provide a better entry level than exit point.

I arrived at the television studio mentally prepared to communicate a coherent stream of thoughts. While I had been on television a number of times, I was nervous, not because of the national audience, but because of what my mind and spirit was trying to reconcile. I kept telling myself that September 11th was just another day, but deep within, I knew that wasn't true. I sat in the green room talking to Senator Chuck Schumer before my segment was scheduled to air, and was impressed by how personable he was. He was a kind man with gentle eyes, I thought to myself, a ray of hope in what was seemingly a hopeless situation.

A producer ushered me to the roof where they were filming, and downtown Manhattan provided the backdrop. A hazy smoke drifted in the background as the putrid smell of burnt flesh and melted steel continued to haunt me. They put a microphone on my lapel and began the countdown. At the last second, they told me they had to cut away for an emergency message from Donald Rumsfeld.

"Hey, if I'm getting bumped, at least it was for the Secretary of Defense," I said as I forced a smile at the producer, hoping that some levity would ease her obvious stress. There were no words in return, no acknowledgment, no eye contact. Everyone was in a state of shock. It seemed like everyone was going through the motions.

I focused on familiar escapes: the markets, our hedge fund, and my writing.

I walked across town and made my way home as volunteers raced toward the still smoldering remains of the World Trade Center. Many of my friends had given blood or assisted the fire department with moral support and words of encouragement, but I never found my way downtown, perhaps a subconscious admission that I wasn't ready to face the newfound reality. Instead, I focused on familiar escapes: the markets, our hedge fund, and my writing.

It's been said that something good comes from all things bad, and while there was no way I could tell at the time, that one thing for me was perspective. It would be a long, painful, and expensive lesson, and one that almost left me littered on the side of the road.

Focusing Anew

The markets were closed for the week following September 11th and that gave Jeff, Matt, and I an opportunity to map our strategy. We knew there would be a process of price discovery since there was no historical context to lean against, and existing paradigms no longer applied. "The market was extremely oversold heading into this event," I told my partners as I pointed to numerous technical indicators. "The selling panic will provide an opportunity to make some savvy purchases." I took comfort in the familiarity of my trading acumen, a lucidity and instinct that I had learned to trust. We would be looking at large losses in our portfolio when the markets reopened, and I knew the first snapshot of our P&L would be ugly.

To make matters worse, our office telephony was severed during the attack, and we had no command center to execute our protocol. Jeff found a space in Rye Brook, an hour north of the city—three hours, when there was traffic—and we set up shop. Instead of eight screens and a telephone turret with direct lines to our brokers, we planned to take on the world with makeshift equipment. It was far from optimal, but it could have been worse—it could have been a lot worse.

The decision was made to forge ahead, and once it was, there was no looking back.

We discussed swallowing a bitter pill once the markets opened and flattening our portfolio, which would have still been up close to 10% for the year. "Ten percent isn't shabby," I said. "Our investors will understand that given what we've been through, we need to retrench before assuming new and different risk."

The decision was made to forge ahead, and once it was, there was no looking back. The market opened the following week and quickly chopped 4% from our gains before our first trade was executed. We fought with everything we had and left it all on the field, before attempting to recover at night. This process was repeated day after day after day.

I didn't want to sleep. Every time I closed my eyes, vivid nightmares jolted me back to a reality I didn't want to accept. The feelings of guilt began to build, which was strangely my predominant emotion. How could I be so upset when others lost so much more? Why did I cry each night after putting on a brave face for my staff and on TheStreet.com? How long would I be able to shoulder this load when I was melting from the inside out?

I wrote columns that expressed my opinion that equities would rebound sharply after the initial plunge, and we operated with the same plan, carefully picking our spots and adding layers of exposure as a function of price. History validated my view, but it took much longer than I expected, and the market fell much farther than I thought it would.

Our performance slid into the mid-single digits and I twisted the knife into myself, wanting to suffer, somehow feeling that I deserved it. Still, as consuming as our losses were, they paled in comparison to the gaping wound that opened in my soul. Someone had once told me that energy isn't created or destroyed, it is simply transferred from one reality to another.

Unbeknownst to me at the time, that process was already in motion.

13

Foul Play

Following September 11th, our makeshift offices for Cramer Berkowitz were located next to a small airport in Westchester. Every time a private jet took off, we collectively flinched as the roar of the engine shook our trading desk. We were riddled with anxiety, but there was no quit in us, despite the freefall that occurred in the market and by extension our portfolio.

I wrote all day, every day, while at the same time, trying to steady our fund and lead our staff. Jeff never said a word about my double duty. He knew that Jim, who was no longer with the fund, wanted me to write, and perhaps that had something to do with his patience.

We were riddled with anxiety, but there was no quit in us, despite the freefall that occurred in the market and by extension our portfolio.

When I wasn't trading, I wrote, and when I wasn't writing, I thought about what to trade or what I should write. I was emotionally terrorized, although at the time I had no idea how damaged I was. I told my readers that we would get through it together, and I carried both roles for a few weeks before it became obvious that it was more than I could bear. I was sleeping three or four hours each night, if that, but given my persistent nightmares, I wasn't sure that was a bad thing.

I had a fiduciary responsibility to my investors and that, more than anything else, prompted me to pick up the phone. I called TheStreet.com editor-in-chief, Dave Morrow and told him we needed to talk. I desperately needed to make a change. "This is difficult for me to admit," I said, "but I can't write ten to twelve daily columns anymore. I give you my word that I'll do whatever I can, but that probably means no more than four to five columns each day."

"Not a problem," he assured me. "We understand and appreciate whatever you can do."

I hung up the phone and felt relieved, yet guilty, since I sensed that my readers might be upset. I went home that night and wrote a heartfelt, honest column called "The Passing of the Torch."

The article never posted, which was the first time that ever happened.

I had written hundreds of articles for TheStreet.com, but that column carried a particularly tender message. I spent hours manicuring the vernacular, combing through each word so that the message would come through loud and clear: I'm here for you, but I will ask for patience as I get my life, my firm, and myself to a place of relative balance and stability. I sent it to the editors and prepared for the influx of e-mails that would arrive the next day. But the article never posted, which was the first time that ever happened.

I called Dave, and he told me that the audience couldn't handle another loss. "They already lost Bill Meehan," he said, referring to my friend and co-columnist who had died in the North tower at the point of impact. "They can't afford to lose you as well."

Fish or Cut Bait

Jim wrote in his first book, *Confessions of a Street Addict*, that I was wildly emotional except when there was money on the line, at which point I was as cold as Saturn. That same mindset applied to my dealings with TheStreet.com when, despite valid reasons for incoherence, I was as lucid as I've ever been. I had given everything I had to that platform and expected some latitude in return. I explained to the editors "This is life. This is the world we live in, and my column should post as it was written." It wasn't simply a matter of respect; it was the right thing to do. I hadn't gone to the bathroom in over a year and a half without communicating to my readership. We had a bond, and they deserved to know the truth.

Morrow wouldn't budge and repeatedly told me that the column wouldn't post. I eventually told him that he had two choices: Publish the column as it was written and I would continue to write whenever I could, or he could axe the column and I would tender my resignation immediately. Dave would not relent, and I weighed his words as I watched the crimson array of flickering ticks on my screens.

"Dave, this isn't about my ego or page views. This is about trust. If I leave, I'm not coming back." I didn't want to resign and secretly hoped he would back down. I could tell the pressure was beginning to get to him. As the editor-in-chief, he was responsible for content and was measured by the traffic it generated. For me—in the midst of multimillion dollar swings, nervous employees, stressed partners, and lost friends—bartering with an editor, who had no leverage because I never signed a contract, wasn't a source of stress.

Publish the column as it was written and I would continue to write whenever I could, or he could axe the column and I would tender my resignation immediately.

"You won't resign," he said confidently. "You want to be the next Jim Cramer!"

"No, Dave," I said matter-of-factly, "I just want to be Todd Harrison."

There was silence as he weighed his options. "Listen," he said, "don't make an emotional decision. This has been a rough couple of weeks for you." He was right, but I didn't respond, opting instead to wait for his next move. "We're not going to run the column. I'm the editor-in-chief; it's my decision and this is what I've decided."

"I quit," I said. "I wish you guys the best of luck."

His response was one that I'll never forget. "Congratulations, Todd, you'll never write in this town again."

I was a pure trader again, and a part of me was considerably relieved by the lesser load.

I hung up the phone, and Jeff and I locked eyes. I was a pure trader again, and a part of me was considerably relieved by the lesser load.

Somewhere in the back of Jeff's mind, I'm certain he was glad as well.

The Jedi Mind Trick

I had only written for a year and a half, but the process was ingrained as part of my daily routine. No matter my mood, regardless of circumstance, and without interruption, I shared my stream of consciousness every session that the market was open. Some days were easier than others, but there was steady consistency; every move that I made and every shift in my outlook was communicated with the world.

My image remained on the Web site above the words "Todd Harrison's Trading Diary" for weeks after my resignation. That bothered me. I wanted a clean break, but I had bigger fish to fry in the form of a bleeding book that suddenly gave back the better part of our hard fought year.

I missed the daily catharsis, but there was plenty to keep me occupied. White powder found in a post office, fresh threats of imminent attacks, those damn planes shaking our office every 15 minutes. It was a freaky sequence of events during a dark time for the world.

My inbox filled with e-mails from concerned readers. I had an unwritten rule that if someone took the time to write, I would respond as a function of respect. As it turned out, those exchanges were the only remaining connection to my audience, a microcosm of the subscribers that had read me daily. I was silenced without so much as an opportunity to say good-bye.

Readers of mine forwarded the exchanges they had with TheStreet.com editors, who had told them I was on sabbatical and would soon return, despite my very clear and definitive departure. I understood why they did what they did. They made decisions they believed to be in their own best interest. It's not what I would have done, but it wasn't my business, and I normally wouldn't get involved. But that was different. While it was their platform, it was my name, and they were my words. I no longer wanted to be associated with TheStreet.com.

True Colors

I called Dave Morrow to vent my frustration and found a new attitude on the other end of the line. "You just need some time to relax," he told me. "Take some time and come back when you're ready." I assumed that he was catching heat for the rift, or perhaps he didn't think I would call his bluff, but it was a moot point. I told him that I don't work with people I don't trust and left it at that, despite the nagging realization that my readers were getting the short end of the stick.

Jim still had influence in our fund, which continued to struggle in the wake of 9/11. Not once during that period did he and I connect— our perceived kinship no longer existed. While our performance was still positive for the year, the slow, steady grind of the fourth quarter took its toll, both on the fund and its stewards.

I didn't discuss TheStreet.com with my partners—they, like I, had more pressing responsibilities. I tried to let the situation settle despite my growing unease with the way it was being handled. Each time I saw an advertisement that promoted "Todd Harrison's Trading Diary," I looked the other way. With every e-mail I got from a concerned reader who asked for the date of my promised return, I internalized the aggravation. I actually convinced myself that I had put the entire experience behind me until I dialed into TheStreet.com conference call when they reported earnings.

After discussing top-line results, CEO Tom Clarke, fielded questions from the audience. Marc Cohodes, a well-known hedge fund manager and a large holder of TSCM stock, finally asked the question that I wanted to hear.

"What happened to Todd Harrison and is he ever coming back?" Tom paused before answering as I sat up in my seat and pressed the phone to my ear. "Todd went through a lot and is experiencing emotional difficulties. We hope to have him back soon."

Trading Places

I was managing a $400 million dollar portfolio through a terrorist attack. The last thing I needed was the CEO of a publicly traded company telling the world that I was emotionally unstable. I tried to focus on trading, but the frustration was palpable as we clung to single-digit returns. After 11 months, we had little to show for our efforts. I still had a base salary to fall back on, but that was supposed to be a buffer. That's the fatal flaw of the Wall Street mindset—the personal high water mark. Once you make five million dollars, anything less feels like a failure. It seems silly now, but when you're thick in the middle of it, it's easy to get caught up in it.

That's the fatal flaw of the Wall Street mindset—the personal high water mark. Once you make five million dollars, anything less feels like a failure.

Insiders at TheStreet.com whispered to me that subscriptions were considerably lower after September 11th, and I couldn't help wonder if some of them were the same people who had written letters to my grandfather when he was sick. I felt guilty—not happy, not validated, not vindicated—but guilty. The welfare of those around me—my traders, my former readers, and my family—weighed heavily on my psyche. And there was the other guilt, the one that constantly questioned how I could feel so bad when others had lost so much more.

I missed my column and the release it provided but didn't admit that to anyone. Instead, I set out to explore alternatives and hoped to find another venue that would take the place of my once stable stage. I craved a new beginning—something, anything, to stop the intense pain that had suddenly consumed me. I needed an escape. Drugs weren't the answer, marriage wasn't feasible, as I had yet to find the "one," and I wasn't about to follow in the footsteps of my father and run away.

I sat awake in bed until 3:00 or 4:00 each morning, sifting through potential solutions in my still frazzled psyched. It was out there, and I was determined to find it.

14

Genesis of a Dream

In the months leading into September 2001, I developed a friendship with a woman named Casey Cannon. She had reached out through e-mail, and I responded, as I typically did to those who took time to write me.

Our connection felt unique from the beginning. She asked the right questions and said the right things. She had been an accomplished player in the entertainment arena, having worked for Industrial Light & Magic with George Lucas before venturing out on her own. Her profile on IMDB (The Internet Movie Database) featured more than 30 films working with the best people in that industry. Casey also knew Jim and his family well—in fact, she produced his retirement video, which caught my attention for the high production quality of the work.

Traders wanted to be famous, and most folks in Hollywood wanted Wall Street's money.

Prior to my Labor Day trip to Maui to see my father, Casey suggested that I stop in Los Angeles so we could meet. She was directing the opening sequence on Cameron Crowe's *Vanilla Sky* and asked me if I wanted a cameo role. Having never been in a feature film, I quickly accepted. The split second shot took ten hours to produce, which pushed my flight to the next day and allowed us some time together.

I mused to her that nobody had ever bridged the chasm between finance and entertainment, and that many traders wanted to be famous, and most folks in Hollywood wanted Wall Street's money. If we could tie education into the mix and create a benevolent experience, it seemed like an intuitive and scalable fit.

I introduced the notion of bringing Hoofy and Boo to life. While the Wall Street bull and bear played globally, nobody had ever put faces or names to them—nobody had ever branded them. Animation was already a generationally accepted genre, as evidenced by the success of Mickey Mouse, Bugs Bunny, and *The Simpsons*. It *felt* right.

While the Wall Street bull and bear played globally, nobody had ever put faces or names to them—nobody had ever branded them.

"If Walt Disney can brand two rodents as cultural icons," I offered, "we can take the Wall Street bull and bear and effect positive change through financial understanding."

Once that thought germinated, it was difficult to shake, and I became obsessed with the concept of creating a place where metaphorical representations of financial dynamics could live in harmony, away from the pitfalls and pain in the real world. I wanted to build the platform, and Casey seemingly possessed the skills to facilitate my dream.

"How much do you think it will cost?" I asked as my flight to Maui was announced.

"Thirty grand, tops," she replied, which sounded reasonable enough. With plenty of money in the bank and fresh pep in my step, my entire perspective shifted. The world suddenly made sense again.

"It'll be a place where Hoofy and Boo will gather to debate the merits of the financial markets," I said as I readied to board the plane. "A platform for discussion, a collection of intelligent opinions, and a community of respected thought leaders...." I paused to think and drew a veiled analogy to a quorum necessary for prayer.

"We'll call it Minyanville."

Familiar Faces

I had discovered that my father was bipolar and later learned my business partner was as well; I lost my best friend Ruby a few months later, and as my grieving began to subside, I watched aircraft slam into skyscrapers as people jumped from the flames. It was a deeply introspective time in my life. It was a turning point, one way or another.

The specter of Minyanville rose like a phoenix from the scorched earth and res ued me from realities I didn't want to face. A breath of life was injected into my lungs. It was an escape, a corridor from a very painful place to a bright, animated world without terror or acrimony or politics or agenda.

I attempted to focus on the fund and tried everything I could to recapture the momentum I once took for granted. Gains were elusive and profits were scarce, the mirror image of the profitable scrimmage we had played the previous year. Everyone goes through slumps, I thought at the time. I was sure that we would bounce back, as we always had.

It was an escape, a corridor from a very painful place to a bright, animated world without terror or acrimony or politics or agenda.

One day in late November, an hour before the close, my phone rang. It was Jim, and it was the first time since I resigned from TheStreet.com that he had reached out to me. My emotions were a mixture of excitement, trepidation, and caution. I clearly didn't know what to expect, but I was happy to hear from my old friend.

"Hey man!" he began with enthusiasm. "I want you to come on my show tonight." Jim was beginning his renaissance as a television personality, co-hosting *America Now* with Larry Kudlow.

"I would love to," I explained, "but I'm not feeling well." It was the truth—I was terribly run-down—but it wouldn't matter. After several circular repetitions of the same conversation, it was obvious that I wasn't going to wiggle out of the spot. "All right," I said, "I'll be at the CNBC midtown studio at 7:00 p.m., and we'll get it done."

As the co-hosts on CNBC bantered about tax stimulus and market psychology, I played my part, smiled, and offered whatever insight I could. When the camera turned toward me, I shared, "Fund managers are chasing performance," in reference to the sharp rally that followed the post-9/11 plunge. "I see it and respect it, but I don't believe it's going to last. Bubbles, in my view, don't end with a V-shaped recovery."

The Morning After

I settled into my turret at 6:00 a.m. the next morning, powered up my systems, and found six e-mails waiting from Jim. They began early in the morning, and I read them in chronological order.

The first was innocent enough, something along the lines of "Hey man, thanks for doing the show." As I scrolled through the correspondence, his tenor and tone shifted. He became increasingly agitated, and by the sixth e-mail, outright rude. I read his final note a few times. "I had you on my show, the least you can do is write a column for TheStreet.com. If you don't want to respond to me, then FINE!"

I wasn't concerned that his internal fires were ablaze, but I didn't want to bite his hand. He still had money in the fund, he still had our investors' ears and, truth be told, I was still indebted to him as a friend.

I told Jeff that I would write a column if it would calm the furor. Maybe it was a legal thing given TheStreet.com had told my readers I was coming back. I don't know, and I really didn't care. I just wanted to make peace with Jim, and move on with my career.

I agreed to write a year-end article chronicling what was and what would be. It was a strong and cathartic column, and while I wrote with the intention that it would be my last article, it reminded me of how much I loved to write, how much I missed the forum. After it posted, Dave Morrow called and asked if we could talk. "Sure," I replied, "swing by tomorrow after the bell."

When Dave got my office, I left my traders on the desk and ushered him to a conference room. Once there, he expressed his regret over what had happened, apologized with sincerity, and asked me to come back to TheStreet.com. I told him that I needed a few days. I knew why he was there and that it had nothing to do with my best interests.

I contemplated his offer and asked for another meeting, this one at a downtown restaurant. There, over a Grey Goose martini, I laid out my thoughts to the top brass of TheStreet.com. "Why don't we partner on a professional product, one that's geared to the hedge fund audience? I'll provide content, you guys run the back-end, and we'll whack up the revenue."

"Great idea!" they exclaimed after conferring. "Let us put our heads together, and we'll get back to you in a few days."

Later that week, we again met, and they laid their cards on the table. "Three percent of the gross revenue," they said. "We'll give you 3% of the gross revenue." I'm not sure what I expected to hear, but I was clearly underwhelmed by their opening salvo.

"I don't think so," I quickly answered. "That's not going to work."

They asked what it would take to get the deal done, and I told them I would get back to them. I returned to my office where 200 positions and an uncertain tape awaited, and tried to focus on the task at hand. While I was surprised by their offer, I knew that was how the game was played.

I spent the rest of the week asking myself some difficult questions and weighing their past transgressions against my desire to again write. When push came to shove, I decided that I was willing to swallow my pride—I wanted to again write my daily column.

I wanted to write for those who had written the letters to my grandfather, and I wanted to write for myself.

I called Dave the next morning and told him that it wasn't about the money, and I was willing to move forward, but I didn't want to just target a professional audience. I wanted to write for those who had written the letters to my grandfather, and I wanted to write for myself.

"We can't do that," he suddenly said. "We can't have our best writer on the old site while we're launching a professional product aimed at hedge funds."

I was prepared for many things, but I was shocked by that latest twist. "We have nothing left to discuss," I said as I hung up the phone, disgusted at myself for being so vulnerable.

They knew it was a good idea, and they were going to launch it with or without me.

Full Steam Ahead

As 2001 ended, my relationship with TheStreet.com died with it. They came back a few times with lucrative offers—a lofty six-figure salary and multiple six-figure stock options—but the numbers didn't register. I knew that if I worked with them again, I would have only myself to blame.

Our fund finished the year slightly above the flat line, and I breathed a heavy sigh of relief that my performance anxiety had a new shelf life. That was the way it worked on Wall Street—the registers were cleared at the end of December 31st and everyone started from scratch.

I was emotionally spent after September 11th, battling the market and discovering the ugly truth behind the digital media landscape. I suffered from post-traumatic stress disorder and fought the demon of depression, although I didn't realize that at the time. Seeing what I saw—the jumpers, the impact, and the fireball—took a heavy, subconscious toll on me.

TheStrcet.com gave my position in their new platform to fund manager Doug Kass, a friend of mine who called me before he accepted. I wished him well and turned my attention closer to home. My primary focus was the fund, where I was entering the second year of a two-year deal. The other was Minyanville, which suddenly encapsulated my hopes and dreams. It was more of a mission than a business venture—it was entirely personal, and very much an escape.

On the weekends and during nights, I worked incessantly on building the wire frames that would bring Hoofy and Boo to life. The $30,000 budget that I communicated to Casey quickly proved conservative. My intention wasn't to build TheStreet.com—my ambition was much larger than that, perhaps grandiose. I envisioned a community that bridged Wall Street and Main Street, a world-class platform that educated, entertained, and engaged. I wanted to change the world, and nothing was going to stop me. Not Jim Cramer, not TheStreet.com, and certainly not money.

I spared no expense. We enlisted the help of John Bell, who was nominated for an Academy Award for visual effects, to illustrate Hoofy and Boo. Casey worked from her Santa Monica home office, and we constructed the Minyanville platform.

I hid from it in Minyanville, which was a parallel universe with cartoon critters. I know it sounds crazy, but I truly believe that it saved my life.

Profits at the fund were elusive, due in equal parts to the new market dynamic and the emotions that were competing for our attention within the office. I awoke at 5:00 a.m. each day and navigated the markets before returning home at night to brainstorm on my vision. Dinners and weekends with friends had to wait. I worked 20-hour days, and whenever possible, locked myself in my apartment, turned off the phone, and closed the curtains. I wasn't aware of the severity of my mental state—I just knew I felt...different.

I hid from it in Minyanville, which was a parallel universe with cartoon critters. I know it sounds crazy, but I truly believe that it saved my life.

The mood within Cramer Berkowitz was tenuous at best as we forged ahead. I wasn't privy to conversations between Jeff and Jim but assumed they were strained. Jim was reinventing himself as a television personality and writing for TheStreet.com. He knew I was in the throes of creating Minyanville and was entirely displeased. Cramer has always needed an enemy to motivate him and would create one if necessary. In fact, he would tell me years later that he believed I built Minyanville to spite him.

I wasn't intimidated, which seemed to agitate him even more. That friction took a toll on our management, particularly after experiencing the horrors of 9/11. The freewheeling fun that was the hallmark of our corporate culture was gone, in no small part because we were no longer beating the Street. Our sudden mediocrity had nothing to do with Jim—I would argue that our firm was more functional without his emotional swings—it was simply a new world, and we were in the middle of a confused conduit of emotions, alliances, and geopolitical agendas. Our innocence was gone, and our country was preparing for war.

Internally, I readied for the exact same thing.

15

The Audible

I worked around the clock, trying to create profits by day and Minyanville at night and during the weekends. I was no longer motivated by conventional measures of success such as money or status—things that had seemed so important to me just a few months prior.

I knew that 9/11 affected me—seeds were planted that day that sowed beneath my consciousness—but hadn't a clue how profound the ramifications were. I internalized my experiences and thought to myself that nothing would ever stop me if I could just power through. *If I could just power through....*

My soul and spirit felt like damaged goods, and I didn't go out much, which was a rapid departure from the active lifestyle I once lived.

My soul and spirit felt like damaged goods, and I didn't go out much, which was a rapid departure from the active lifestyle I once lived. My friends reached out, but who had time for that? There was too much to do, or that was my internal rationalization when I opted for a few hours of sleep when I stopped working. Eventually, my phone stopped ringing, and social invitations dried up. I barely noticed.

I couldn't continue at that pace and didn't want to. I remember looking into the mirror one morning and not recognizing the drawn, empty face that returned my stare.

I knew the financial markets and I loved my grandfather— Minyanville and the Ruby Peck Foundation were the only solutions that made any sense.

I had started a children's foundation in my grandfather's name, and I wanted to extend that sense of purpose to my career. I didn't want my headstone to one day read, "He had a good feel for the tape." I knew the financial markets and I loved my grandfather—Minyanville and the Ruby Peck Foundation were the only solutions that made any sense.

It had quickly become an expensive reality, one that ultimately cost millions of dollars, but once I began to pave that path, there was no turning back. The hours turned into days, the days into weeks, and the weeks into months. Before I knew it, I was staring at the final stretch of 2002. It was almost time to reset the clocks.

Houston, We Have Liftoff...

We launched Minyanville.com in October 2002 as a "financial infotainment and education" platform.

TheStreet.com chose that exact day to open their Web site for free as we pulled back our curtain. I knew they were watching, but I underestimated their agenda. I had reached out to them before we launched, offering my content for free as long as it was branded Minyanville. Their response was essentially, "Go fuck yourself—you're the enemy now." They were ruthless, but they weren't idiots. The last thing they were going to do was lead my readers directly to me.

I searched TheStreet.com Web site and realized they had deleted most of my content from the archives. Countless travails from the inner elasticity of the bubble, personal reflections about my grandfather, steadying words to investors on how to position for the new world—all gone.

Cramer took some of his money out of the fund, and I could tell he was leaning on Jeff. It was a tough spot for my good friend, and the stress was evident. Imagine working with someone you genuinely love, a person who chose you to facilitate his success, only to become a source of angst instead. I resented Jim for that. Whatever was going on was between us, but he had leverage with our investors, and used that influence to turn the screws on my partner.

By December, we were tired and fried after yet another year of battle. Our 2002 results mirrored those of a year earlier, marginally positive gains and well below what we were capable of doing. And we were miserable, which is an unpleasant dynamic in any environment, but an absolute barrier when battling for performance in the fierce world of finance. If you're not on the same wavelength as the guy next to you, you won't shoot straight when performance is in your sights.

Just as Jeff and I communicated without words while trading, we had a similar connection away from the tape. He was equally aware that our relationship was strained. He had Jim on one side, our investors on the other, and a staff that relied on us both to put food on their table in the middle.

He, like me, wore his heart on his sleeve, and I could see it beating a mile away.

Exit Strategy

The conversation started as any other, with me asking him if we could get off the desk and chat. When we shut the door to his office, there was a silence that spoke volumes about what needed to be said. I don't know how the conversation would have gone if I hadn't started it, but I imagine the outcome would have been much the same. It was one of the most honest and heartfelt discussions we ever shared.

As partners, we knew what needed to be done, but as friends, we were saddened that it came to that.

"This isn't working," I began as we looked into each other's eyes. "I agree," he responded, quicker than I anticipated.

As partners, we knew what needed to be done, but as friends, we were saddened that it came to that. He knew that I was building Minyanville, and deep down, I knew it wasn't fair to put him in that position. Writing while trading was a great idea when your partner owned the company and performance was pristine, but it was entirely different when you're viewed as competition and profits are elusive.

In the former situation, it's a seamless dynamic, and in the latter, an unnecessary distraction.

Twenty minutes later, I tendered my resignation. After fifteen years of friendship and three years of blood, sweat, tears, and laughter, we decided that we would part ways.

After fifteen years of friendship and three years of blood, sweat, tears, and laughter, we decided that we would part ways.

It was the middle of December—almost three years to the day after we uncorked those bottles at Gramercy Tavern—and I suddenly had no idea where I was going to operate from. That's a problem when you've already spent a million dollars on a Web site that was predicated on mapping the financial markets.

For the first time, the reality of the situation hit home. I had three weeks to relocate, and two of them were already booked at an expensive resort in Bora Bora. I took my trading team to dinner that night and assured them they would be taken care of, although I was less sure about myself.

In a few short weeks, I would need a new home, and I hadn't a clue where that would be.

Blink and You're in Business

It didn't take long for the word to spread. Wall Street is a small place when it comes to juicy news. Our trading coverage—from Goldman to Morgan to Bear Stearns to Lehman Brothers—lined their pockets with commission revenues generated by Cramer Berkowitz, a number that grossed between $90 million to $100 million per year during my tenure at the head of the desk. They weren't happy that the gatekeeper was relinquishing the keys to the castle, particularly when the castle did business the right way.

Minyanville had launched, I was the only writer, and the Ruby Peck Foundation had proven costlier than anticipated. I needed a home that allowed me to stay in the flow and make some dough, and after 12 years on the Street, I had peers who had a vested interest where I landed.

I listened to a few offers, unsure of which direction to pursue, when a former colleague asked to meet with me before I made any decision. He worked with a reputable money manager at a fund located on Park Avenue and as part of their business model they operated a "hedge fund hotel," providing space, trading systems, and human capital in exchange for order flow and trading commissions.

I walked to their offices and was immediately impressed with the large marble lobby that housed some of the world's largest financial institutions. I made the rounds, sat with the principal players, and listened to possible collaborations. "You should think about starting your own fund," they said. "We'll set you up here and help with the process and paperwork."

It wasn't something I had seriously considered, but they were friendly faces with a solid structure. And they believed in me, which wasn't something I overlooked.

I had faith in my abilities and plowed most of my money into the fund.

Minyanville was costing almost six figures per month on top of my initial investment, and I had numerous other obligations. Furthermore, the effort required and the costs to start a not-for-profit foundation after 9/11 were substantial. I needed a revenue generator, something that could underwrite a symbiotic ecosystem for all three endeavors. I had honed my skills at Morgan, sharpened them at Galleon, and demonstrated them at Cramer Berkowitz, building one of the finest desks on Wall Street. As I listened to the potential hedge fund structures, my mind began to calculate the windfall.

A typical structure charges 1% of total assets as a management fee and 20% profits as a performance fee, but they floated something differently, a structure with no management fee and 50% payout of the profits. It was a deal reserved for the best traders on the Street, a back-end loaded payday based purely on performance.

They offered to seed me, and while I wasn't particularly thrilled about launching a new fund, the offer was too good to refuse. I had faith in my abilities and plowed most of my money into the fund. Others followed, and before I knew it, I had moved my personal items and sports memorabilia to my new Park Avenue home.

16

The Abyss

I felt...free. The stress of a multimillion dollar hedge fund manager—the outsized risk, the sleepless nights, the battling over positions, the gains and losses, my self-worth defined by a bottom line each and every night—wasn't something I was going to miss.

I was only 34 years old, but I had aged well beyond my years. I remember thinking that I had made a "lifestyle decision," that the new routine of managing a smaller fund, building Minyanville, and running the foundation would facilitate an easier and more relaxing existence.

As the capital management paperwork went through the proper channels, I traded my personal account to keep my skills sharp, and with the help of a single assistant, squirreled away sizable gains. It was unfamiliar operating without a team, but it didn't impede my success, as evidenced by my initial results. I took calculated bets, and I was rewarded handsomely; my confidence grew—maybe I was that good and the terms of my new fund were warranted after all?

Minyanville transitioned to a pay site—$10 per month to help offset the operational costs—but it remained a loss leader. I received stacks of bills to pay each week and signed them quickly. I grew tired of seeing my name on the bottom of a check rather than in the middle of it. I needed an income generator, a final piece of the puzzle that would tie it all together. My fund launched in March 2003.

It was a tense time in the world as the US and UN danced around the prospects of war. I was certain the worst was yet to come, that an invasion of Iraq would plant seeds of geopolitical instability, and that the financial engineering I witnessed at Morgan Stanley would ultimately unravel. Perhaps I was still emotionally damaged from the terrorist attacks, but as I watched "Shock & Awe" on CNN, I thought to myself, "This is the end of the Roman Empire—this is a tipping point through a historical lens."

I believed that a cumulative comeuppance would overwhelm the markets and the derivative foundation would prove destabilizing.

My fund opened for business almost to the day of the invasion, and I established bets against the market. I focused my attention on Fannie Mae, Freddie Mac, and the financial supermarkets that were disguised as banks. The finance-based economy was littered with derivatives, and the leverage in the system was already massive. It was an opportunity to start my venture with a bang, and I was eager to morph my experience into performance.

The stock market rallied sharply as policymakers injected fiscal and monetary stimuli. The real estate bubble took shape, and the elasticity of the credit bubble began to expand at an astonishing rate. The Federal Reserve made a massive bet that if they bought time and pushed risk further out on the time continuum, a legitimate recovery would take root, and the economy would ease back toward a normalized business cycle.

I didn't buy it. I believed that a cumulative comeuppance would overwhelm the markets and the derivative foundation would prove destabilizing. I didn't foresee a spirited recovery following the carnage of the technology bust, and I anxiously put my money where my mouth was.

I was wrong. Rising asset prices fed on themselves, and consumer psychology shifted from a fear of losing into a fear of missing. I underestimated the motivation of the Federal Reserve, and badly miscalculated the timing of the eventual comeuppance. I had used higher prices to double down on my downside bets and wrestled with a harsh and humbling reality—I had become emotionally attached to my positions. I post-rationalized my losses and lost any semblance of discipline.

The stakes had never been higher, and as I looked around the table for the sucker, I couldn't help wonder if that sucker was me.

I wasn't used to losing and took it very personally. I shared my increasingly unpopular view on Minyanville and defiantly scaled into fresh short positions as a function of time and price. I expected the equity market to suddenly awake to what was happening in the world, but it continued to shrug off negative news and digest any hint of supply. I felt very small; every day was a painful reminder of how wrong I was, and my failures were broadcast in real-time for the world to see.

The hedge fund that was supposed to underwrite the collective costs of my various endeavors instead lost large sums of money, and while I had some cash stashed away, most of it, including my entire retirement account, was at risk alongside my investors.

The stakes had never been higher, and as I looked around the table for the sucker, I couldn't help wonder if that sucker was me.

The Other Side of the Trade

I was mired with losses, consumed with relative performance, overwhelmed with overhead costs, completely miserable during the day, and helplessly sleepless at night. I pressed harder, worked longer, traded faster, wrote more—it was the only solution that made any sense. Surely, if I worked harder still, I would be rewarded for my efforts.

I pressed harder, worked longer, traded faster, wrote more—it was the only solution that made any sense.

As the year progressed, I put everything that wasn't directly related to my professional efforts on hold. I worked around the clock, my social life was a ghost town, and I was edgy and angry at my lack of success. The toys that were once a validation of my happiness served as empty reminders of misplaced priorities.

I always believed that I was humble, particularly in a business where humility was viewed as a weakness, but then I was bare. My fire—the energy that ignited my hopes and dreams—was damp and dark as I delved deeper into depression.

If you look for happiness in a bank account, you're missing the bigger trade.

Lou Mannheim famously said, "Man looks into the abyss, there's nothing staring back at him. At that moment, man finds his character. And that is what keeps him out of the abyss." I've had many swings during my career—$20 million to $30 million swings in a single session—but it wasn't until 2003, as my savings and resolve dissipated, that I truly got it.

I won't say that money is insignificant—that's untrue—but I can share from experience that if you look for happiness in a bank account, you're missing the bigger trade. I didn't find what I was looking for when I seemingly had it all. In fact, it took losing almost everything I had to understand what true wealth really is.

The private jets and front-row shows morphed into calls not being returned by those I had helped succeed. David Slaine told me to expect it, but I didn't foresee the magnitude or suddenness. Friends on the Street, those who benefited from my free-flowing, revenue-generating ideas, disappeared when I needed them most.

I wasn't naïve enough to think that I would be treated with the same standing, but I projected my loyalty to people and places where it didn't belong. My circle of trust tightened, slowly at first but then dramatically, as I mentally let go of those who bit the hand that once fed them.

If I couldn't deliver it, I was no longer part of it.

Socially, a similar dynamic began to take shape. Invitations became scarcer when there weren't free drinks or fancy rides. The other side of the bigger, better thing was a painful reality to absorb—if I couldn't deliver it, I was no longer part of it.

Full Circle

In May 2003, I arranged for my father to return to the East Coast for the first time in almost 20 years. While I was consumed with trying to save my personal ecosystem, I had made him a promise when he was in jail two years prior and gave him my word. While I was losing everything else, I wasn't about to lose that too.

One year after Adam and I ventured to Hawaii with hopes of saving our dad, I returned, as I said I would, to enjoy his freedom with him. After his long stretch of homelessness and hopelessness, he had been properly medicated and was in a healthy place. It was then that we discussed his trip to the East Coast and before I knew it, he touched down in New York City.

As I greeted him, we embraced in a long hug that melted away years of disappointment, anger, and judgment. He was a humbled man, the type of humility that comes after you've lost everything and stared into a different type of abyss—that of life.

At times during the week, as we walked through the streets of Manhattan, I turned around to find him sitting with the homeless comparing notes. It was an odd sight to see, but it was strangely enlightening, and I've never looked at the homeless the same way since.

He told me that during his years of solitude and desperation, the glimmer of his children sustained him. He cried openly as we talked for hours upon hours, and I realized that we both had our demons, and everyone has their struggles.

A few days later, we traveled to Baltimore, and my father met his grandchildren for the first time. As we sat around the dinner table the first night, I found myself watching him with an unfamiliar sense of pride. It was the first time I experienced that particular emotion—after a childhood of seeking his approval, our roles had somehow reversed.

I'm unaware if he knows the gift that he gave me when he traveled to see his children and grandchildren.

I thought back to the time Adam and I spent in Maui—the blood smeared on the jail cell, the orange jump suit, the pandering for loose change, and how our father broke down and told us there were times he no longer wanted to live. I knew that when all of that was happening, he felt that he had no way out, but he managed to persevere and get himself back on track.

I'm unaware if he knows the gift that he gave me when he traveled to see his children and grandchildren, but watching him that night at the dinner table strengthened my personal resolve at a time when I most desperately needed it. I wasn't sure how I would turn my life around, but I knew one thing—if there was a way, I was going to find it.

The Driftwood and the Perfect Storm

I scrambled for redemption, tangible or otherwise, but the harder I tried to find my footing, the deeper I fell into the crevasse of despair. As the markets ripped higher, my losses dove into double-digit territory. It was the mirror image of the success I experienced in

2000, and that wasn't lost on me. The cycle of life, I thought to myself; *the other side of the cash register.*

Most of my money was in the fund, losing value alongside the capital that investors entrusted to me, and that, coupled with my substantial investments in Minyanville and the Ruby Peck Foundation, had quickly chewed through my life's savings.

When I started the year, I had millions of dollars in the bank, but that quickly evaporated, and when the tide didn't turn, it became clear that decisions needed to be made. If I tried to keep all those efforts afloat, everything would drown at once.

There was palpable heartache, and I visited a cardiologist, certain that the pain my chest was a foreboding sign. "You have to take better care of your health," he told me. "Get some exercise and stop putting so much pressure on yourself."

With each passing day, I swallowed more water, and with each wave of losses, my breath became more labored.

I tried to tell him about my metaphorical critters named Hoofy and Boo that were going to effect positive change through financial understanding, but he didn't seem to care. He was more concerned about my ability to physically continue. In my mind, death was the only thing that would stop me.

The Minyanville community, while loyal, was still relatively small. Our mission of provoking thought and providing education through a vicarious process—as opposed to offering outright advice to a faceless audience—was a departure from traditional financial media and entirely unconventional in what was then an immediate gratification world.

With each passing day, I swallowed more water, and with each wave of losses, my breath became more labored. I was so focused on conventional measures of success that I lost sight of why I started Minyanville in the first place. I lost sight of who I was.

The sad truth was that there wasn't much money—or time—left.

I had to make difficult decisions as I edged toward the end of 2003. They weren't decisions of choice; they were decisions of need. The business that was supposed to underwrite my existence and the one that sustained my soul couldn't coexist if I hoped to survive another year.

If you do what you love, the money will come. That's what I told myself when I stepped down as president of a $400 million hedge fund, and I reminded myself of that as I struggled through the final months of 2003.

The sad truth was that there wasn't much money—or time—left.

The Fork in the Road

I huddled with my advisors and tried to identify a potential solution. Given the cash burn in Minyanville, they told me I would be insolvent in a matter of months. It had been almost a full year since I decided to create my new professional existence, and the well was almost dry.

We spent countless hours trying to map strategies that would allow my dream to survive. My team believed in me, but they were lucid and pragmatic, and they saw how fragile I was, a shadow of the once powerful hedge fund master who moved markets and made millions. I was close to my break point and everyone knew it.

"I'm not going to abandon Minyanville."

"What are you going to do?" they asked as I studied my bank statements, hoping that they would magically change.

"I'm not going to abandon Minyanville," I told them, knowing full well that it wasn't an option. "I've still got money hidden away, and I'll use that until we succeed."

They sat in silence staring at me, unsure of what to say.

"Build it and they will come," I said in my best Kevin Costner voice, trying to convince myself that I knew something that they didn't, but they weren't as optimistic. I was bleeding from every orifice, day after day and night after sleepless night. They were right, but I didn't see another option.

"If I'm going down, I'm going down with my best one-two punch, and those are Minyanville and the Ruby Peck Foundation."

I had spoken with my investors throughout 2003, and the final call didn't come as a surprise. They knew the risks before they invested, but that did little to quell my guilt, shame, and pain. I had let them down and lost their money, an unavoidable reality that haunts me to this day. For some strange reason, having most of my money in the fund made me feel better, not worse.

If I ran out of gas, there would be nobody left to tow me home.

I closed the doors, returned the remaining money, and booked the largest loss of my professional career. It remains the single biggest black mark on the name and word of Todd Harrison, a painful and embarrassing chapter in my life. The road to recovery would be long and hard, and I had to power the engine with a small reserve fuel tank.

If I ran out of gas, there would be nobody left to tow me home.

17

The Phoenix

I began 2004 the way I started every year, trying to learn from the past and turn my mistakes into lessons. I told myself that I would give Minyanville twelve months to succeed, or it would leave a legacy as a seven-figure hobby that emptied my bank account.

We built a stable of writers, respected professionals such as Tony Dwyer, Scott Reamer, Kevin Depew, and John Succo, who shared their insights online with "Minyans" around the world. They didn't do it for the money—I couldn't afford to pay them—they wrote because they believed in effecting positive change through financial understanding.

I would give Minyanville twelve months to succeed, or it would leave a legacy as a seven-figure hobby that emptied my bank account.

In the summer of 2004, we hosted an event called "Minyans in the Mountains" in Crested Butte, Colorado. The intention was to bring our online community to life, put faces to names, and offer an engaging forum for financial intelligence.

Among those attending was my best friend and college roommate, Kevin Wassong. After standing on the periphery since I founded Minyanville, Kevin wanted to see what I was doing firsthand. He had been a steady sounding board as I forged a path into an entirely new industry and had offered sage advice on how to position a next-generation digital media platform.

If anyone knew that space, it was "Fish." After graduating from Syracuse, Kevin went to Hollywood to pursue his creative ambitions before returning to New York. He launched the digital group at J. Walter Thompson and in 1998, became CEO and built it into a top-ten interactive services company.

Kevin had been responsible for a lot of firsts; he brought Sotheby's first auction online and ushered Merrill Lynch and NASDAQ into the digital advertising space. To him, Minyanville was the "big idea" that could connect generations in the financial vertical and transcend media platforms. He arrived early to help me tend to the last-minute details and prepare gift bags for the guests. That was Kevin, he never cared about the money or the summer homes—he was never the "bigger, better thing" guy.

The fledgling community that assembled in the mountains was proof positive that our vision was indeed vibrant.

As we roasted s'mores at the Saturday night bonfire, I allowed myself a rare moment of satisfaction. After three years of heavy lifting and almost unbearable stress, Minyanville had arrived at a place of collective consciousness despite a motivated agenda and dwindling funds. The fledgling community that assembled in the mountains was proof positive that our vision was indeed vibrant.

As we watched the sunset over the mountains and laughter filled the air, I turned to Kevin and we shared a smile. That's when I knew he saw it, too.

Of Mice and Men

They say that if you told an entrepreneur how much work it would take for his or her dream to succeed, they would never start the business in the first place.

My schedule was brutal; I awoke at the crack of dawn and wrote about the structural shifts in the financial markets with a forward-looking lens, while trying to juggle capital raises, business development, and philanthropic endeavors. Do what you love and the money will come? I continued to remind myself of that despite the nagging realization that passion wouldn't pay the bills, and my bank account was almost empty.

Kevin and I met at an Applebee's near his home in Larchmont following the summer of 2004. There, over beers and cheeseburgers, we scribbled the "wagon wheel" business model on the back of the check. The central hub was Minyanville and the "spokes" were ancillary business lines, including advertising, subscriptions, licensing, events, video games, entertainment, and merchandising. It was indeed a "big idea," and while there were preexisting theme brands— ESPN in sports, or Discovery networks in science—there was no roadmap in the financial vertical for what we were about to endeavor.

When I landed a meeting with Stan Gold—Roy Disney's business partner—in California in the autumn of 2004, I asked Kevin to help put together a presentation and join me for the trip. We prepared visuals and collateral—a video trailer, posters of Hoofy and Boo, MV cookies and valuation metrics—but they had been delivered to the wrong office in Southern California. We got word of that as we pulled up to Stan's office, 15 minutes before our scheduled meeting. That's when Kevin turned to me and said, "The show must go on!"

We were told we had 30 minutes of Stan's time, but once there, three and a half hours into the presentation, and after our packages finally found their way to our meeting, we pounded the table with passion and purpose.

"You don't see it, Stan," I said in a hurried voice, pleading with him to see what we saw. "If Walt Disney can take two rodents and create cultural icons, we can take the Wall Street bull and bear and effect positive change through financial understanding!"

Stan, sitting at the far end of the conference room table wasn't convinced. "You sure have chutzpah," he said as he weighed our words. "Why don't you circle back when the company is more mature?"

While we didn't "get the order," something shifted within Kevin during that presentation, and by the time we got back to New York, he and I decided to raise money and give Minyanville an honest shot.

The final months of 2004 were a furious push to pull together a private placement memorandum and the proper documentation. We huddled with lawyers, met with accountants, and presented to potential investors, many of whom failed to see what we saw.

I swallowed the bills and looked through the costs, opting instead to channel every ounce of energy into fulfilling our mission.

With the holidays bearing down, it was almost time to reset the clocks.

Mexicali Blues

The excitement of mapping a tangible plan commingled with the fear of an unspoken reality as I hosted a holiday gathering at Rosa Mexicana restaurant in New York.

I was, in many ways, going through the motions of a confident leader. My body was there and my instincts acute, but the work was excessive, even by my standards. My heart hurt, my muscles ached, and my head throbbed. I remember splashing water on my face in the bathroom and whispering, "This can't be healthy" before feigning a smile and returning as the host.

I was scheduled to go to Tucson the following morning, as I desperately needed to unplug from the unbearable marathon that was my life. I felt as if I was running from something for so long and at such a furious pace, I didn't know any other way to operate.

I still wasn't aware that I suffered from a deep depression following the events of September 11; those feelings were buried somewhere deep within me, perhaps protecting me from a consciousness I didn't want to—or couldn't—face.

My grandfather had once told me to never run scared.... My dream had a shot at survival, but the future was anything but certain.

After 14 years of forging a professional identity, one that directly shaped my self-esteem, my perceived success was no longer measured by the speed of a car or the watch on my wrist. I knew that my priorities had changed, and deep down, the thought of spending a week alone scared the hell out of me. I wrote about the importance of balance and the necessity of perspective on Minyanville, yet my words dripped with hypocrisy—my tank was empty and the anxiety consuming.

My grandfather had once told me to never run scared, and I reminded myself of that as I made my the way to the airport. My dream had a shot at survival, but the future was anything but certain.

Desert Storm

In my search for success, I had ignored that the purpose of the journey was the journey itself, and I forgot that by the time I arrived at where I thought I wanted to be, the journey would have already ended.

My programming was so deeply ingrained that I rarely stopped to question it. I was trapped by self-imposed expectations and continually reset my internal bar so that it was always out of reach. I believed that allowing myself to feel was a weakness if it competed for my attention.

When I arrived in Arizona, I immediately participated in activities. The grounds of the hotel were littered with couples and groups, but I mostly kept to myself. Mountain biking, weight lifting, hiking— I did anything I could to occupy my mind and avoid the inevitable introspection.

Still, from the moment I opened my eyes to my last thought each night, I wrestled with who I was, how I lived, and what my purpose was. By the time I started dissecting one thought, a new one replaced it. My head spun for days as my thoughts viciously collided with each other.

In my search for success, I had ignored that the purpose of the journey was the journey itself.

One afternoon, I paced my room and tried to make sense of my emotional crosscurrents. I wandered to the patio that overlooked the foothills in the far distance.

Without realizing it, I hopped the ledge and began to walk.

There are instances in each of our lives that are defined by a moment of clarity, and I can count them on one hand.

I remember jogging in the islands after my Morgan Stanley promotion, standing atop a cliff overlooking the clear, blue water.

There was a moment in Maui the week before September 11, watching the sunset on the horizon and making peace with my father.

And there was that day in the desert on a random Tuesday afternoon. I was so engrossed in my own thoughts that I didn't remember when or why I started walking. An hour or so later, I was in the middle of nowhere, as I tried to find answers to the questions that I had never thought to ask.

As I looked to the sky and spoke aloud to my grandfather, trying to sort through the disparate aspects of my existence, tears formed in my eyes. Minutes later, I began to weep uncontrollably. I couldn't remember the last time I cried, but it was measured in years, not months.

September 11. Losing Ruby. My father's abandonment. Leaving a high-paying professional perch. The battles with established media. Chewing through my life savings.

Ruby

September 11

Uncertainty

Doubt

Abandonment

Money

Faux friendships

Ruby

The thoughts sped quicker and quicker as I stood in the empty desert. I turned around to make sure I knew where I was; I wasn't quite sure I did. I was confused, angry, sad, lonely, bitter, and empty all at the same time.

There was comfort in being able to define my experiences, but that safety came with the cost of containment.

Without warning, the clouds opened and cried alongside me. The rain furiously beat me with the rat-tat-tat of tiny bullets, and I immediately felt sorry for myself. I absorbed nature's wrath as if I somehow deserved it, wallowing in my own self-pity. "Perfect!" I screamed loudly in defiance. "Bring it!"

I looked down, around, and back down at my feet, which were firmly planted in the desert sand, and suddenly realized that I was in a safe place. I inhaled deeply and again looked to the sky. I squinted through the rain, saw through my obvious troubles, and realized how truly lucky I was. At that exact moment, I connected with the person I had lost years earlier; I found the friend who had been missing since before September 11.

The rain consumed me, I raised my arms in the air and my head fell back. I felt a smile creep on my face as I let go of the pain and strain of my internal burdens, and a ray of sunlight peeked through the clouds and kissed me on the cheek. I was certain that it was my grandfather, putting his hand on my shoulder, telling me to think positive—that "this too shall pass."

I had always been spiritual, but that was different. It was a sign.

Something very powerful shifted within me that day. When I walked into the desert, I operated from a position of finality. At 35, I saw who I was, what I had made, where I had been, and whom I was with. There was comfort in being able to define my experiences, but that safety came with the cost of containment.

I didn't have a financial cushion, my business was unproven, my future was uncertain, and there were real risks in my life plan.

By the time I arrived back in my hotel room, there was a tangible sense of release, as if I had released my demons, left them in the desert, and arrived at a new beginning. Rather than obsessing about what was, I felt extremely blessed to have the opportunity to shape what could be. I didn't have a financial cushion, my business was unproven, my future was uncertain, and there were real risks in my life plan.

But what did I feel? Gratitude. Immense, complete, absolving gratitude.

18

The Journey

I've long believed that the definition of professional nirvana is to do what you love with people you respect while serving the greater good.

Kevin and I raised money at the beginning of 2005, and we built out the entire wagon wheel. Hoofy and Boo staked their claim as the Wall Street bull and bear, our loyal community grew in size and scope, The Ruby Peck Foundation raised seven figures for children's education, and I got to work each day with my best friend.

Life was good, which isn't to say that it was easy. Building a business always takes longer, is much costlier, and consumes more energy than originally anticipated, particularly when swimming against the steady stream of the conventional wisdom that financial intelligence must be dry and homogeneous.

Do what you love with people you respect while serving the greater good.

We remained true to our mission of effecting positive change through financial understanding, even if that message wasn't particularly pleasant. In the years that preceded the financial crisis, we monitored the cumulative imbalances that lurked beneath the seemingly calm surface, warned of "a prolonged period of socioeconomic malaise entirely more depressing than a recession," and opined that the financial industry was technically insolvent.

Those observations are obvious with the benefit of hindsight, but it was a lonely stance when the Dow Jones Industrial Average was trading near all-time highs. Through it all, we shared our views with a consistent thread of humor and humanity; we stayed true to our voice—we stayed true to who we were.

We weren't immune to the financial stress, but we persevered—we believed.

In retrospect, the timing of Minyanville, while serendipitous for those who absorbed our content, was somewhat ironic. I had invested millions in a financial literacy platform that educated people from the ABCs of personal finance to the 401(k)s of to how to interpret the markets, our team worked tirelessly at building the infrastructure and organization, and BOOM—the crisis arrived just as we began to take off.

We were in the final stages of numerous business development endeavors when everyone—and everything—went dark. Minyanland—our massive multiplayer online game that teaches children how to earn, spend, save, and give—was suddenly viewed as an unconventional marketing expense. The Fox Business Network, which launched "Hoofy & Boo's News & Views" in 2007, took a harder news angle and cancelled our contract a year later. Despite our record online traffic, advertising cycles had shortened from months to weeks.

In short, we weren't immune to the financial stress, but we persevered—we believed.

The Envelope, Please

We were informed of the Emmy Award nomination on the very same day that our show had been cancelled. "New approaches to financial and business reporting," I said to Kevin, hoping to lessen the sting of the loss. "This has our name all over it."

When we walked through Manhattan on the way to The Rainbow Room, I looked toward the sky and rubbed the gold "Ruby" bracelet that my grandmother had given my grandfather for their 40th wedding anniversary. He was with me, much like he had been that day in the desert; his hand was still on my shoulder, and the sunlight still on my cheek.

We were informed of the Emmy Award nomination on the very same day that our show had been cancelled.

As representatives from The National Academy of Television Arts & Sciences handed out the glistening statues, the tension steadily grew. It may have been a material possession, but I would be lying if I said that it didn't matter to us.

Bill Small stepped on stage and said, "Our next category honors some of the more creative examples in business and financial reporting being broadcast over the air and on the Web today."

They showed video clips of the three nominees—CNNMoney.com, Minyanville's World in Review and Newsweek.com—before Mr. Small continued.

"The vast majority were not network entries that were nominated but newspapers and magazines who are doing remarkable work on the Internet—television on the Internet, excellent work—so to my colleagues at CBS, NBC, ABC, and CNN, you might take a look at that and see why they get nominated and you don't."

He began to unseal the envelope and my heart stopped beating.

"The Emmy for new approaches to business and financial reporting goes to...Min-e-yan-ville.com."

I shot up from my chair and planted a kiss on Kevin's cheek, and the next few seconds blurred as I found myself on the podium.

"I am Todd Harrison, the founder and CEO of Minyanville, although at this point I feel like a cross between Sally Field and John Belushi in the cafeteria scene in *Animal House*."

I took a deep breath; I was overwhelmed with emotion.

"You know, they say that a dream is only as powerful as those who believe in it, and it is with humility...that I accept this on behalf of not only our team and Kevin Wassong, and everybody up here and the partners who believed in us, but the entire Minyanville community around the world that believes that we can effect positive change— and we will effect positive change—if we stick together in this world."

I paused, trying to maintain composure for one more sentence.

"And...to my grandfather Ruby," as I kissed the Emmy and held it toward the sky, "this is for you."

We were ushered off stage toward the photo gallery. Bill Small smiled as he stepped back to the podium, and said, "I wonder if anyone is left in the office? Their president gave me his calling card with pictures of Hoofy and Boo, who I expect don't have executive positions."

I didn't hear the laughter from the crowded room. As soon as I stepped off the stage and navigated through the kitchen toward the pressroom, I collapsed into the first corner I found, closed my eyes, and began to cry.

Bringing It Home

There are now Minyans in 229 countries and territories that drive upwards of 10 million page views each month, and our content continues to inform, educate, and entertain. We've never viewed ourselves as a conventional media property, and that may be precisely what's needed during these particularly unconventional times.

Minyanland, the online gaming platform for children, has almost 600,000 registered kids and 300,000 registered parents, and discussions are underway to bridge the virtual world utility into real world savings. Hoofy and Boo—our animated critters that serve as metaphorical representations of the stock market—still stream an endless supply of smiles. Now more than ever, a little levity goes a long way.

I don't make the type of money that I once did on Wall Street, but the psychic income has never been higher.

Someone once said that the only difference between a business and a job is whether you need to be there each day for it to function. Minyanville is entirely bigger than any one person—I am a lone voice amongst a strong community—but I genuinely enjoy getting out of bed each morning and believe in my heart that we've only just begun to stretch our legs.

I don't make the type of money that I once did on Wall Street, but the psychic income has never been higher. As the ramifications of the longstanding societal largess and the implications of public policy manifest, we continue to help millions of Minyans shape their perceptions, priorities, and principles of financial awareness online, each and every day.

While giving a speech at a university a few years ago, after being introduced to the audience, someone asked which professional accomplishment I was most proud of. I wasn't prepared for the question, and the answer left my lips before I realized it.

While in business it pays to be an animal, in life it pays to be yourself.

"My failures...they tested my resolve and capacity. While I once measured myself by a bank account and a business card, I discovered that real success is staying true to who you are and being grateful for what you have. Once I learned to view obstacles as opportunities and problems as possibilities, everything shifted in kind."

I'm a different man now than when I chased the cash register—which isn't to say I don't enjoy money. I've simply found that what you do pales in comparison to how you do it regardless of what it is you choose to do.

And while in business it pays to be an animal, in life it pays to be yourself.

Acknowledgments

While profitability begins within, my relationships have paid the greatest dividends. To that end, this story would not have been possible without numerous people for whom I'm compelled to express my heartfelt gratitude.

I must thank Kevin Wassong for his unbelievable friendship, support, and guidance over the last quarter-century, and for being the best man, save Ruby, that I've ever met.

My sincere appreciation is extended to all the people who have contributed to the development of Minyanville, as well as our incredibly talented team that proves each day that a dream is only as powerful as those who believe in it. Your efforts to create something truly unique, distinctive, and game-changing in the financial media sphere have helped millions of investors around the world make better decisions, and yes, smile.

I would like to acknowledge Jeanne Glasser, my fantastic editor, for allowing me to be myself throughout this process, even though I wasn't always easy, and the entire crew at FT Press for getting behind this project.

I am further indebted to those who helped shape my path: David Slaine, John Succo, Jack Skiba, Tommy Carden, Chuck Feldman, Joel Pollack, Harry Silver, Len Spivak, Jeff Berkowitz, Matt Jacobs, Brooks Johnson, Bruce Fredrickson, Loretta Barrett, Allan Millstein, Kevin Depew, Chris Dixon, Dan Englander, Peter Atwater, Smita Sadana, Tom Eggers, Judith Dornstein, Fil Zucchi, Larry Kramer, Adam Heine, Tony Dwyer, Bill Meehan, Charlie Mangano, Pete Moses, Casey Cannon, Bobby Sager, Jeff Saut, Bennet Sedacca, Matt Ford, Jeff Macke, Dave Callaway, and, yes, Jim Cramer, for opening a door I never knew existed.

I would like to express my love to those who have profoundly affected my personal journey: my mother, Carole, for all she's done and who she is; my brother, Adam, for being my best friend; my sister-in-law, Faith, for being awesome; Maia and Bradley, my uniquely special niece and nephew; my grandmother, Dorothy, for being the hippest chick in south Florida; and my father, Steve, for showing his true colors before it was too late.

I must also thank Jamie, the most amazing woman I've ever met, for allowing my dreams to come true; my daughter, Ruby, who is due to arrive as this book is published; Gavin and Mug, for inspiring me to be a better man; and Phoebe, Crash, and Blue, for putting love in my heart.

And to the entire Minyanville community that visits us daily on www.minyanville.com, I'm profoundly grateful for your continued support as we find our way through this most interesting world. Without you, there would be no us.

About the Author

Todd A. Harrison, founder and CEO of Minyanville Media, Inc., has 20 years of experience on Wall Street. He spent 7 years on the worldwide equity derivative desk at Morgan Stanley as Vice President, was Managing Director of Derivatives at The Galleon Group, and was President of the $400 million hedge fund Cramer Berkowitz. He has appeared on FOX, CNBC, CNN, and Bloomberg TV, and in *The Wall Street Journal, BusinessWeek, The New York Times, Worth, Fortune, Barron's, Dow Jones MarketWatch, New York Magazine*, and Canada's *National Post*.

Todd has lectured at numerous academic institutions, including Harvard University, Syracuse University, New York University, and The Wharton School at the University of Pennsylvania. He has also been active in research of financial market learning tendencies among college students, and was a contributing author to "Threat, Intimidation, and Student Financial Market Knowledge: An Empirical Study," published in the *Journal of Education for Business*.

Todd was featured in the 20th anniversary documentary of Oliver Stone's movie *Wall Street* and in 2008, he received an Emmy Award from The National Academy of Television Arts & Sciences for his role as Executive Producer of *Minyanville's World in Review*, the first and only animated business news show.

INDEX

FINANCIAL TIMES

In an increasingly competitive world, it is quality
of thinking that gives an edge—an idea that opens new
doors, a technique that solves a problem, or an insight
that simply helps make sense of it all.

We work with leading authors in the various arenas
of business and finance to bring cutting-edge thinking
and best-learning practices to a global market.

It is our goal to create world-class print publications
and electronic products that give readers
knowledge and understanding that can then be
applied, whether studying or at work.

To find out more about our business
products, you can visit us at www.ftpress.com.